Instructional Strategies for Teaching Content Vocabulary, Grades 4-12

Instructional Strategies for Teaching Content Vocabulary, Grades 4-12

Janis M. Harmon
Karen D. Wood
Wanda B. Hedrick

National Middle School Association
Westerville, Ohio

International Reading Association
Newark, Delaware

National Middle School Association
4151 Executive Parkway, Suite 300
Westerville, Ohio 43081
NMSA® www.nmsa.org

INTERNATIONAL
Reading Association
800 BARKSDALE ROAD, PO BOX 8139
NEWARK, DE 19714-8139, USA
www.reading.org

Sue Swaim, Executive Director
Jeff Ward, Deputy Executive Director
Edward Brazee, Editor, Professional Publications
John Lounsbury, Consulting Editor, Professional Publications
April Tibbles, Director of Publications
Mary Mitchell, Designer, Editorial Assistant
Dawn Williams, Production Specialist
Mark Shumaker, Graphic Designer
Lisa Snyder, Graphic Designer
Marcia Meade-Hurst, Senior Publications Representative

Photo Credits: J. Lounsbury, J.J. Hayden

Library of Congress Cataloging-in-Publication Data

Harmon, Janis M., date-
    Instructional strategies for teaching content vocabulary, grades 4-12/Janis M. Harmon, Karen D. Wood, Wanda B. Hedrick.
        p. cm.
    ISBN: 1-56090-192-6 (pbk.)
        1. Vocabulary--Study and teaching. I. Wood, Karen D. II. Hedrick, Wanda B., date- III. Title.

LB1574.5.H37 2006
428.1071--dc22   2006043302

Acknowledgements

As with any endeavor, many voices are involved who have contributed in varied ways to the completion of this project. As teacher educators, we wanted to be sure to seek out the expertise and helping hands of fellow teachers, existing and former students who work on a daily basis with the students for whom this book is intended. We would like to thank the following teachers representing many school systems and universities: Kimberly Fodge, Charles Van Houten, and Mitzi Sprado from the University of Texas San Antonio; Rebecca Kavel, Melissa Kurek, Katie Keller Dugan, Megan Roland Torgerson, Jeanie Marklin, and Gwendolyn Atkinson from the University of North Carolina Charlotte and Charlotte-Mecklenburg, Cabarrus County and Mecklenburg Catholic Schools in North Carolina; and Ted Banton, Linda Tuschinski, and Peggy Clark from the University of North Florida, Duval and St. Johns Counties in Florida.

We also want to offer a special thanks to John Lounsbury, Ed Brazee, and Mary Mitchell of National Middle School Association and the editorial staff at the International Reading Association, two organizations with wonderful, supportive professionals who have endless ideas and creativity to turn pages upon pages of text into finished books.

Dedication

...to my husband Phil and my sons Phillip and Joseph   J.M.H.

...to my children Eric, Ryan, Lauren, and Kevin   K.D.W.

...to my ever growing family,
Stan, Jenny, Matt, Emily, Stephanie, Adam, Kim, and Jeremy   W.B.H.

Contents

List of Strategies

Foreword

Many years ago, when I began teaching high school social studies, I realized that many of my students had very limited knowledge of the vocabulary that each unit presented. So I did the only thing then that I knew to do. I listed the next chapter's key terms on handouts, provided blanks next to each term, distributed one list per student, and guided everyone down to the library to locate and record definitions. Needless to say, issues ensued:

"What's wrong with saying that the *constitution* means *the way in which something is constituted*? That's what the dictionary says."

"Look, I wrote everything the dictionary had about each word. See how full my worksheet is!"

"This is boring."

As I began to discover then—and as the professional literature now makes clear—having students simply copy dictionary definitions is not a productive approach to vocabulary instruction. To learn vocabulary well, youth require meaningful settings and extensive opportunities to interact with words and the ideas they represent. Youth learn vocabulary best when they exemplify the links among related words and when they analyze the sources and meaningful parts of words. Youth learn vocabulary best when they portray word meanings artistically and dramatically and form connections among words, their lives, and what they are studying. And youth learn vocabulary best when they monitor their proficiencies and when they examine subtleties of word usage, noting multiple meaning words, figurative language, idioms, and so on. When I reflect on my early years teaching vocabulary, I wish I had a copy of *Instructional Strategies for Teaching Content Vocabulary, Grades 4-12*. Then I would have had ready access to productive approaches to teaching and learning vocabulary.

This volume's description of sensible vocabulary instruction is especially welcome these days. Educators long have known that youth require access to new, sophisticated words; but with the National Reading Panel sanctioning vocabulary as one of the five components of reading, educators now are emphasizing it more and more. Additionally, students whose home languages are not English and who come from poverty are leading educators to realize the particular urgency of word learning. This urgency is compounded in the upper-grade subject areas like mathematics, science, and social studies where the concept loads are staggering and the requirements for precise meanings are stunning. Today's educational policy makers also are emphasizing the significance of vocabulary. For instance, the reading framework for the 2009 National Assessment of Educational Progress calls for a vocabulary assessment. Teaching and learning academic vocabularies across the curriculum now are imperatives. The time is right for a book such as this.

A resource that also presents vocabulary strategies distinctively and accessibly is welcome. A flurry of books devoted solely to vocabulary has been published recently. Indeed, my university library's subject holding for *Vocabulary—Study and teaching* contains twelve entries published since 2000. Googling *Vocabulary—Study and teaching* generates 5,970,000 links. This text stands out from the crowd partly due to its accessible, no-frills format. The vocabulary strategies' descriptions, suggested variations, content area examples, and blackline masters are especially convenient. Users of this text will find its strategies to be handy.

A comprehensive resource, one that compiles wide-ranging vocabulary teaching and learning strategies as this volume does, is to be valued. This text groups numerous strategies into reasonable categories and arranges them smartly in chapters and chapter sections. I found in these pages several of my long-standing, favorite strategies (e.g., Concept of Definition Maps, Graphic Organizers), some strategies that I've been advocating only recently (e.g., TOAST, Zooming In and Zooming Out), and some that were unknown to me (e.g., Forced Associations, Typical to Technical Approach). You probably will have similar findings.

Finally, vocabulary development has many moving parts. Among other things, entirely new terms continually enter our discourse. I like to highlight this movement by citing the American Dialect Society's annual Word of the Year results that draw attention to notable new terms such as *podcast* and *blog*. Furthermore, the complexities of subject matter words to be learned differ substantially according to the predictability of their spellings (*dry, desiccate*) and the concreteness of their referents (*end, endergonic*). And youth come to school with quite different aptitudes, attainments, and predispositions relative to word learning. Vocabulary instruction that responds to this commotion is essential; *Instructional Strategies for Teaching Content Vocabulary, Grades 4-12* goes far in framing appropriate responses.

— David W. Moore
Arizona State University

Words and the Ideas They Represent
—the Heart of Content Learning

In the world of television several decades ago, Art Linkletter hosted a show in which he captured the idea that "kids say the darndest things." More recently, Bill Cosby has amused us with hilarious lines uttered by innocent youngsters, and various publications have included funny things that kids say. For example, the *National Review* article entitled "56 B.C. and All That" (March 1, 1993), is a collection of historical bloopers made by students, such as "Socrates died from an overdose of wedlock" and "Ancient Egypt was inhabited by mummies, and they all wrote in hydraulics." As teachers, we can certainly add to these entertaining anecdotes with students' responses to what we sometimes think they are learning in our classes. Here are some that we have collected:

- A young lady in a world geography class had to write a paper about the Greek culture and mentioned that the class system in this culture included "science, social studies, math, and English."
- An eleventh grade English student wrote an essay analyzing the complexity of the development of one character in *The Scarlet Letter.* She wrote "Dimmesdale is an *enema* (for *enigma*) that must be examined closely."
- In a health class one girl misunderstood the teacher's use of the term *diagram* for *diaphragm.*
- When a high school literature class read the play *Inherit the Wind,* a student continually referred to the witness for the "prostitution."
- Several high school students in an American history class thought that the *inherent* powers of the Constitution were powers *inherited* from England.
- In an English class several students thought that an *appositive phrase* was *a positive phrase.*

While our first reaction is to chuckle at these bloopers, we sober quickly when we realize that our students sometimes misconstrue or misunderstand words in our lessons. These episodes really drive home the point about the importance of language and, more specifically, the importance of the words we use to convey ideas to students. We tend to associate vocabulary instruction with English and reading teachers, but as all middle and secondary teachers know, learning new words is at the heart of conceptual understanding regardless of grade level or subject area. In fact, it is impossible to separate vocabulary learning from the development of a sound knowledge base in any content area, as words are simply labels for concepts (Vacca & Vacca, 2002). However, with a focus on teaching the critical concepts in your field, you may not have easy access to the most current vocabulary research that has been conducted in the areas of language development and literacy development. Given this situation, this volume, *Instructional Strategies for Teaching Content Vocabulary, Grades 4-12* is a compilation of research-based strategies to help you, as a middle or high school content area teacher, with vocabulary instruction in your classroom.

In this introduction we address three important questions: (1) What does research say about vocabulary teaching and learning in the content areas? (2) What are the features of content vocabulary instruction? and (3) How do I use this book?

What does research say about vocabulary teaching and learning in the content areas?

Research studies dealing with vocabulary teaching and learning have made clear that

- Knowing a word fully is a continuous process.
- Wide reading is a critical venue for learning new words.
- Direct instruction plays an important role in vocabulary learning.
- Integration, repetition, and meaningful use are critical features of effective vocabulary instruction.

In their review of research on vocabulary, Baumann, Kamenui, and Ash (2003) concluded that objectives for a comprehensive vocabulary program should include: (1) teaching students how to become independent word learners; (2) providing instruction for specific word meanings; and (3) helping students learn to appreciate the multiplicity of words and enjoy using new words.

These objectives underpin vocabulary teaching and learning across a multitude of contexts, grade levels, and subject areas. They also provide guidelines for planning instruction. They represent the basic foundation from which teachers can make critical instructional decisions that support students' vocabulary development. It is at this point, however, that we need to consider the finer distinctions between what it means to support vocabulary learning with narrative texts in language arts and English classrooms in contrast to what it means to support vocabulary learning with expository and informational texts in content area classrooms. While we agree that there is great overlap in practices for both situations, we take the position that each area represents unique cognitive demands and knowledge-specific dimensions that shape the nature of instruction.

The types of words teachers select for instruction with narrative texts may represent crucial ideas related to understanding a character's motive or to grasping the nature of plot events.

The targeted, unfamiliar words may also be tangential to understanding the basic framework of the story itself. That is, in narrative readings many unfamiliar words may be peripheral to following the plot of the story, and, as a result, students may get by with simply a generalized understanding of a term enough to keep comprehension intact.

In contrast, the demands for teaching vocabulary in your content area differ in both nature and task. Vocabulary words are at the heart of learning in content areas because new terms represent the concepts being taught. In fact, you will probably agree that it is sometimes difficult to discern where vocabulary instruction begins and conceptual instruction ends. So students need to acquire a thorough understanding of terms in order to build a foundation for further learning about a particular topic. This represents the continuous nature of word learning and indicates the necessity of helping students refine and broaden their knowledge of discipline-specific concepts (Blachowicz & Fisher, 2002).

What are the features of content vocabulary instruction?

In our investigation of what it means to teach vocabulary across the different academic disciplines, we noted that although instructional practices can vary widely, teachers must still consider the specific nature of selected terms, the situated context of the terms, and student learning ability. To support teachers when selecting appropriate vocabulary instructional activities, we developed a list of features that reflect the issues previously described. The features include the following: *integration, clarification, identification, linguistic attention*, and *metacognition*. While these features can be broadly interpreted and applied to narrative texts, we specifically define the features in terms of the vocabulary instructional demands for the content areas.

Integration. Integration is central to content learning. Just as the phrase "no man is an island" indicates the interconnectedness and relationships we have with one another, the same can be said about words. Words cannot be taught in isolation; they must be taught in relation to other words. Moreover, schema theory supports the teaching of words in semantically related groups, because we learn new words and information about a topic based upon what is already familiar to us (Nagy, 1988). Because many content words are semantically related, instruction that supports vocabulary learning through integration will enable students to make appropriate connections needed for conceptual understanding. Specifically, both categorizing tasks and activities that show relationships among ideas support the feature of integration. For example, a social studies lesson about the exploration of the New World incorporates the

> ### INTEGRATION
>
> Could you teach a unit on the Great Depression without talking about the New Deal, Franklin Delano Roosevelt, and soup kitchens?
> How can you explain the commutative property in mathematics without talking about the numerical operations of adding, subtracting, multiplying, and dividing?

feature of integration when students participate in activities that connect the New World concept with such people as Ponce de Leon and Christopher Columbus.

CLARIFICATION

What happens when a student becomes confused with multiple meaning words, such as legend, spam, or complementary angles?

What do you do when a student does not understand phrases, such as "is consistent with," "can be transformed into," or "is adjacent to"?

Clarification. This feature encompasses two areas that may cause confusion for students: contextual factors that give rise to multiple meanings of words, and procedural vocabulary found in technical readings. First, examining the context in which words appear is critical to word learning, especially in the content areas where familiar words can take on different and unfamiliar meanings. Johnson (2001) argues that teachers need to teach students to expect that words will have multiple meanings, especially when they appear in different content areas. Multiple meaning words enable students to develop both depth and breadth of word meanings that will serve them well across different contexts. Multiple meanings of words are especially problematic for English Language Learners who may not even know any English words for a concept. In addition, students need explanations of procedural vocabulary used in technical readings, phrases that indicate the relationship between and among concepts. In many instances, we overlook common terms and phrases when asking students to read content area texts. Some students may not understand the connective terminology for signaling specific relationships among ideas. Again, this is especially difficult for English Language Learners as these words are not necessarily concrete and therefore become roadblocks to text comprehension.

Identification. Many content specific words are terms representing people, places, and events. Students need ways of identifying and remembering these names. They need to associate these terms with their existing knowledge and with appropriate concepts that may be newly acquired. While these associations are closely related to the integration feature, some students who struggle with reading and remembering may need more support and multiple opportunities to identify people, places, and events. This can also be achieved through visualization strategies and mnemonic devices to trigger memory recall and to reinforce new learning.

IDENTIFICATION

How can you help students develop a mental picture of what happens when two chemicals interact with each other?

In what ways can you help students remember specific terms associated with science lab procedures?

Linguistic Attention. Students can learn many content words by attending to affixes and Greek and Latin roots. Given that approximately 60 percent of words contain recognizable units of meaning (Nagy & Anderson, 1984), especially words used in the sciences, it is important for content teachers to incorporate this feature in their vocabulary instruction. Examining word parts makes learning new words more memorable and enables students to independently figure out the meanings of new words in context (Gunning, 2004). Furthermore, the meanings of prefixes, suffixes, and roots remain constant across different subject areas. This area may actually provide an advantage for many English Language Learners whose first language may be derived from the Romance languages with similar roots or cognates. In addition, English Language Learners may have a heightened metalinguistic ability and may express great interest in studying parts of words for meaning.

> **LINGUISTIC ATTENTION**
>
> Would knowing the meanings of common roots or morphemes, such as centi means "one hundred," help students understand other word meanings, such as percentages, centigram, centigrade, centimeter, or bicentennial?
>
> It is useful to help English Language Learners in your classroom attend to cognates, such as computadora, calculadora, matematica, agebra, biologia, and astronomia.

Metacognition. Similar to other areas of learning, students' awareness of their own learning in different content areas is important. They can become more metacognitively aware of how they learn new content vocabulary by learning monitoring techniques. Self-selection strategies and self-assessment techniques will enable students to more closely examine their own learning and progress in different subject matter areas. Furthermore, students will become more aware of themselves as content learners and will acquire the task knowledge needed to complete work in particular content areas. They will have as well the necessary strategies for monitoring their own meaning constructions as they interact with new words and concepts.

> **METACOGNITION**
>
> What does it take to help students develop independent word learning strategies that apply to content area reading?
>
> How can students take an active role in building and assessing their own content-specific vocabularies?

How can you use this book?

We have developed a user-friendly and practical compilation of strategies for teaching vocabulary that can easily be applied to instruction in any content area. We have divided the chapters by content vocabulary features to help you focus on the type of word learning tasks that are involved in the terms you have selected to teach. A variety of teaching techniques are provided for the five content vocabulary features identified above. Each strategy includes a brief overview of its purpose, content areas that lend themselves to this strategy, and a list of materials. This information is followed by a description of the procedures to follow, suggested variations of the lesson, and content area examples of the strategy.

The majority of these teaching tools are useful procedures for helping all students learn about discipline-specific concepts. However, some techniques will be particularly effective with students who struggle with reading, especially English Language Learners and others who lag behind in reading proficiency. For example, instructional strategies for connecting and relating ideas, such as "Vocab-O-Gram" and "Possible Sentences" (found in Chapter 3) work well in small groups where struggling readers can receive peer support. In addition, the instructional strategies for identifying and remembering terms enable students to engage in visual imaging, such as "Talking Drawings" and to use mnemonic devices, such as "Letter Strategies" to aid in retention of ideas (Chapter 5).

The amount of instructional time varies for each strategy. We refrained from providing specific time frames because of the many factors that determine how long a lesson takes. Some activities can take as few as 15 to 20 minutes whereas others may extend to two days. For example, the "Zoom In and Zoom Out" activity (Chapter 3) can be used as an entire 50-minute lesson or it can be spread across two or three days. On the other hand, emphasizing "Procedural Vocabulary" (Chapter 4) may be embedded in your content lesson where you simply flag these phrases and mention them in class discussions. Additionally, since we know vocabulary knowledge is an integral factor in comprehension, some of the strategies require that teachers integrate the vocabulary throughout the lesson by pre-teaching terms before reading, highlighting them during reading, and reviewing the terms after reading in order to support the learning of overall concepts and content. Another instance of this variability in purpose, timing, and integration is the "Preview in Context" strategy (Chapter 4). This strategy is a means of pre-teaching significant terms before reading by engaging students in a dialogue to scaffold their understanding. Consequently, it is difficult to ascertain the amount of time these student-teacher interactions would require before you feel comfortable proceeding with the actual reading of the content. Keep in mind that timing is always predicated upon your teaching goals and your assessment of your own students' needs, because the vocabulary teaching techniques in this book are designed to support conceptual learning.

We encourage you to use this book as a reference source for lesson planning as you address the critical role that vocabulary plays in content area learning. On a lighter side, we circle back to the beginning of this chapter to the vocabulary "bloopers." While these comments tickle our funny bone because we have the necessary background knowledge to appreciate the humor, our students need and deserve to have a clear and accurate understanding of words and concepts so that they too can chuckle with us whenever a "blooper" comes along.

— 2 —

Planning a Content Lesson with a Vocabulary Focus

Because vocabulary is closely tied to conceptual learning, we believe that instructional decision making about vocabulary will accomplish the goals and objectives that you have for your students. In this chapter we present an outline for a structured lesson design with options for supporting vocabulary learning as one way to achieve specific content learning objectives. The basic format of the lesson follows instructional ideas advocated by Beck, McKeown, and Kucan (2003) for teaching general vocabulary words to students. They have provided guidelines for selecting words, introducing new words, and developing meaningful use of the words as students become more knowledgeable about the targeted concept(s). With struggling learners in mind, we have broadened these guidelines to include the following steps for a content vocabulary lesson:

1. Decide on the conceptual ideas for the unit or lesson.
2. Read the text and develop a word list of related terms and phrases.
   Consider how these terms represent the conceptual ideas students need to learn.
3. Examine the word list to determine how the terms should be taught.
4. Develop activities to introduce, build, and refine the word meanings and phrases before reading.
5. Develop activities to support word meanings during reading.
6. Develop activities to extend and reinforce word meanings after reading.
7. Develop content-specific activities.

We describe each step and provide an example with the term *air pollution*. We have also included a blackline master (p. 15) to use in your content vocabulary lessons.

1. Decide on the conceptual ideas for the unit or lesson

As a content area teacher, you are well aware of the specific topics and concepts that are part of the curriculum in your field. This first step is actually the same one you always take in planning a new lesson. In our example on the topic *air pollution*, the conceptual ideas follow:

- Air pollution has a detrimental effect on people and is a serious threat to the environment.
- Air is polluted by man-made contaminants that are mostly harmful gases.
- Preventive measures must be taken to maintain clean air.

2. Read the text and develop a word list of related terms and phrases

One of the first steps in planning a content lesson is to carefully examine the vocabulary associated with the concepts to be taught as well as other special terms and phrases that are used in text passages that students will read. As a starting point, we recommend that you follow Beck, McKeown, and Kucan's (2003) suggestion to begin by listing all terms and phrases that you believe students may find difficult. Because it is difficult and almost impossible to teach a long list of words, the next step is to narrow the list using the following questions as guides for selecting the most appropriate vocabulary words:

- What words are essential for conceptual understanding?
- If you have a particular theme in mind (e.g., in an English class, you may want to focus on terms that describe the main character in a short story), what terms are critical to the theme or topic?
- Are there procedural terms (e.g., phrases such as "distinguish between") in the list that you need to clarify for students? Set these words and phrases aside for special instruction.

For our example of air pollution, we have the following word list of related terms and phrases:

toxic	ambient air	vapor
smog	atmosphere	contaminants
ozone	dust	detrimental
greenhouse effect	chronic	aquatic life
radon	carcinogenic	consisting of
sulfur dioxide	emission	makes up less than
carbon dioxide	fossil fuels	contributes to
carbon monoxide	soot	reduce the capacity of

While this list of 24 words and phrases appears to be too many words to teach, it actually represents terms that students will learn over the course of a unit on air pollution. Furthermore, it may be sufficient for students to have a general idea about a term rather than a thorough understanding. For example, it may suffice for students to know that radon is a harmful gas found in the basements of homes, without knowing all the specific characteristics and chemical composition.

3. Examine the word list to determine how the terms should be taught

Once you have selected the conceptually loaded terms, analyze them to determine what is probably the most effective way to present them to the students. To do this analysis, consider the following questions:

- Which words represent concepts that will probably be unfamiliar to the students and will likely require special attention and much teacher support?
- Which words are new labels for familiar concepts and therefore easier to teach?
- Which words contain known parts, such as prefixes or roots, and offer opportunities for developing and reinforcing students' independent word learning strategies?
- Can the selected terms be categorized in ways that will make sense to the students?
- Are there variant forms of the words that may be confusing to struggling readers?

Using the above questions, we analyzed our word list for air pollution and noted the following:

- The following terms may be difficult conceptually for struggling readers and will require additional teacher support: *ambient air, carcinogenic,* and *greenhouse effect.*
- Students will probably have some background knowledge about *smog, soot, toxic,* and *fossil fuels* and will need less support for understanding these terms.
- *Sulfur dioxide, carbon dioxide,* and *carbon monoxide* all contain "oxide," meaning a compound of oxygen.
- Because grouping words into categories can help students note how words and ideas are semantically related, we developed the following categories with our word list:

Substances in the air	Processes	Descriptive words	Procedural terms
smog radon sulfur dioxide carbon dioxide vapor ozone dust carbon monoxide soot	greenhouse effect	ambient air chronic carcinogenic detrimental	consisting of makes up less than contributes to reduce the capacity of

- We also noted that any writing or discussion about pollution could include the use of the following word variations:

pollute	polluted	pollutants
pollutes	polluting	pollutive

4. Develop activities to introduce, build, and refine word and phrase meanings before reading

Because there are many ways to introduce, build, and refine new word meanings, we provide several options for this section of the lesson plan. However, it is important to keep in mind that students will have varying levels of knowledge about the terms ranging from full knowledge to no knowledge. Some students may even have misconceptions and wrong assumptions about terms. We provide examples of the Knowledge Rating Chart for assessing students' background knowledge, suggestions for presenting an unfamiliar term, and the use of the KWL Chart, meaningful prompts, and word walls.

Knowledge Rating Chart. Have students complete a Knowledge Rating Chart (Blachowicz & Fisher, 2002) about the selected terms as a tool for assessing what students already know about the concept. This technique is described in more detail in Chapter 7 (see p. 142).

	I know this term.	I think I know this term.	This term has something to do with…	I do not know the meaning of this term.
air pollution				
toxic				
smog				
ozone				
greenhouse effect				
radon				
sulfur dioxide				
carbon dioxide				
carbon monoxide				
ambient air				
atmosphere				
dust				
chronic				
carcinogenic emission				
fossil fuels				
soot				
vapor				
contaminants				
detrimental				
aquatic life				

Suggestion for presenting terms. Begin by asking students what they know about the term. If some students indicate a fair understanding of the term, then have the class brainstorm associated terms. A prompt could be the following: When you think about air pollution, what comes to mind?

If students do not know the term, then provide a definition and a context.

DEFINITION: Pollution is any action that makes something unclean or unhealthy. Specifically, air pollution is any action that makes the air we breathe unclean or unhealthy.

CONTEXT: Show pictures of polluted air in a smog-filled urban area.

KWL Chart. A KWL Chart (Ogle, 1986) is effective for placing the student in the center of learning. In chart format, students indicate what they *know* about a topic, what they *want* to know, and subsequently what they *learned* by the end of a lesson or reading. The KWL chart can be used to help students consider what they know about air pollution, to generate questions about air pollution, and to set up a purpose for reading about air pollution. An adaptation of the KWL chart developed by Huffman (2000) includes several focus questions.

	What are the causes of air pollution?	What impact does air pollution have on people and the environment?	How can we prevent air pollution?
What do I know?			
What do I want to learn?			
What have I learned?			

Meaningful Use Prompts. It is important that students be given many opportunities to use newly learned terms in meaningful ways instead of just providing definitions. One technique is to use prompts such as the following:

Gases that are *toxic*:

Health problems that can happen to people because of *air pollution*:

Word Walls. Word walls have become common in middle level classrooms. These visual displays of words for a unit are very important especially for English Language Learners who need the visual support for learning new words and concepts. For the *air pollution* example, a word wall can contain related terms as well as pictures of terms, such as a smog-filled urban area with the term *smog* written under it. Display the words in semantic clusters rather than alphabetically so students can quickly make connections between the word meanings and the appropriate concepts.

5. Develop activities to support word meanings during reading

To support students as they read

- Specifically direct students to pay attention to the words and terms discussed in class as they read.
- Have students make notes about what the author is saying about the term.
- Have students write questions about what the author is saying when the term is used.

6. Develop activities to extend and reinforce word meanings after reading

Once students have some understanding of the conceptual terms, they then need opportunities to use the terms in meaningful ways. It is through multiple and varied activities that students internalize the meanings of words and their understanding of concepts. Many of the activities described in this book provide support for helping students acquire these understandings. The options mentioned below only represent the numerous possibilities available to assist students in their learning of new concepts and words.

- Ask meaningful questions, such as the following: (adapted from Beck, McKeown, & Kucan, 2003)

    Can *smog* be *toxic* to people?

    Would a large city have more *air pollution* than a small town?

    Does the *greenhouse effect* explain how tomatoes can grow well in planters?

    Can *radon* be found in a school building?

- Ask students to complete sentences, such as the following:

    Many large urban areas frequently have *smog* problems because …

    Sulfur dioxide, a smelly, colorless gas emitted when *fossil fuels* are burned by industrial factories, is detrimental to people because …

    Air pollution is also *detrimental* to *aquatic* life because …

- Have students create a semantic map that shows how the terms are interrelated (see Chapter 3 for a discussion on semantic maps). Use the software program *Inspiration* to create the map (see Figure 1).

- Based on the category topics listed above, have students create concept circles as described on p. 58 in Chapter 3.

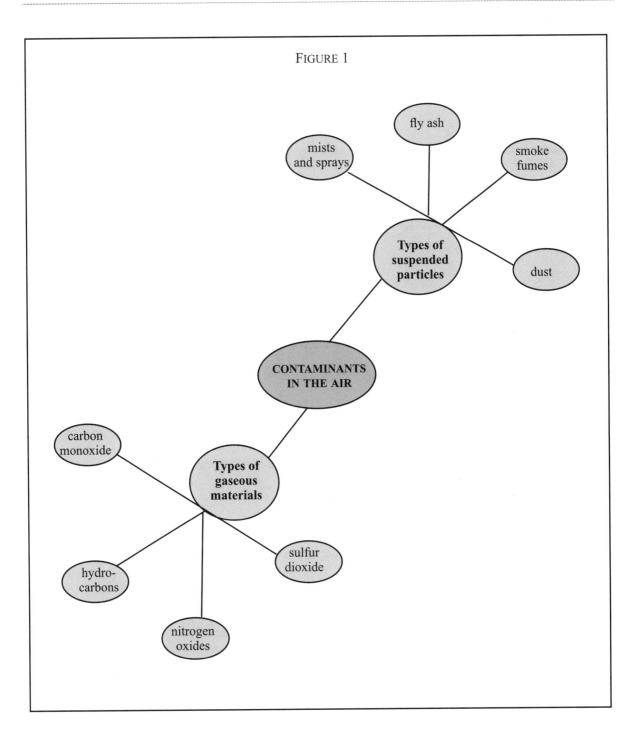

FIGURE 1

An *air pollution* example follows:

Shade the section that does not relate to the other words. Then name the concept.

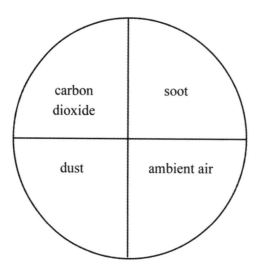

- For clarification of the procedural terms listed above, provide an explanation of each phrase and an accompanying example related to something that is familiar to the students. For example, with the phrase "makes up less than," tell students that there are 12 girls and 15 boys in the class. Then say, "So girls *make up less than half* of the total number of students in this class." Chapter 4 contains more suggestions for teaching procedural vocabulary.

7. Develop content-specific activities

The final step in planning involves engaging in activities that support the application of newly acquired conceptual knowledge and includes the meaningful use of newly learned words associated with the concepts. Activities can include examining dust particles under a microscope, finding magazine pictures of smog-filled cities and bumper-to-bumper cars on the highways, or conducting lab experiments that measure the effects of sulfur dioxide on plants. The students can think of activities. These activities provide rich opportunities for students to use new terminology as they participate in class discussions or debate political issues surrounding air pollution. Furthermore, students can use the terms as they engage in writing activities that report their findings of lab experiments or share their own personal views about solutions to air pollution.

(Blackline Master)

VOCABULARY PLANNING SHEET

Conceptual ideas to be taught	
Word list representing conceptual ideas	
Ways to teach words	
Before reading activities to introduce, build, and refine word meanings	
During reading activities to support word learning	
After reading activities to reinforce and extend word meanings	
Content-specific activities	

Instructional Strategies for Teaching Content Vocabulary, Grades 4-12, by Janis M. Harmon, Karen D. Wood, and Wanda B. Hedrick. Published by National Middle School Association and International Reading Association. Copyright 2006 by National Middle School Association.

Connecting and Relating Ideas

onceptual understanding is at the heart of content learning. Students learn many concepts in a variety of content areas throughout their time in school. While words themselves are simply labels for concepts, many words are needed to explain and describe a concept (Vacca & Vacca, 2002). Students develop a deeper understanding of concepts when they are able to understand and make connections among related ideas. This chapter focuses on the integration of vocabulary and concepts as an approach for helping students develop the necessary connections for learning new ideas. Some strategies highlight the importance of categorizing in conceptual understanding and others enable students to see relationships among ideas. The 13 strategies described in this chapter are identified below.

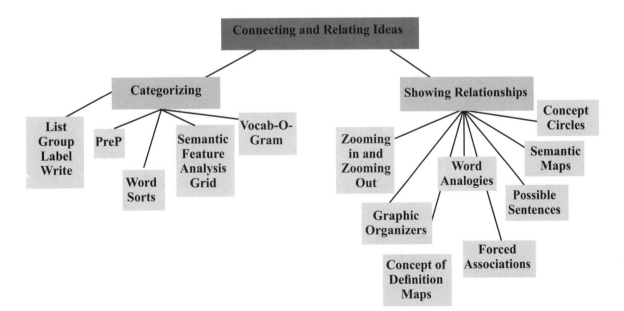

LIST-GROUP-LABEL AND WRITE

List-Group-Label and Write helps students use prior knowledge to improve their vocabulary, comprehension, and writing. During this brainstorming-type activity students are asked to recall as many terms as possible on a given topic and then group the terms according to their similarities. The List-Group-Label and Write strategy will
- Help students use and improve their vocabulary.
- Promote the brainstorming of ideas.
- Help students classify and group terms or concepts.

Materials
A passage from text or other resource to be read during the class session.

Content Areas
All

Procedure
1. Select a topic related to the current unit of study about which the students have some prior knowledge.
2. Select a passage on the chosen topic which the students can read within the class session.
3. Ask the class to think of everything that comes to mind on the topic. Display these terms and concepts on the board or an overhead transparency. This is also an appropriate time to introduce or pre-teach any significant terms.
4. Either as a class or in small groups, have the students group or categorize the terms displayed. The students may also be asked to explain why they chose to put certain words or phrases in a particular category.
5. Engage the class in any other background building activities (e.g. watching a brief video clip, viewing pictures or demonstrations related to the topic).
6. Then ask the students to read the selected passage.
   a. Have students share what they have learned about the topic after reading the selection. Display these associations as in Step 3. (Some of the terms mentioned previously may be repeated to validate what the students knew before reading.)
   b. Again, have the students group and classify the terms displayed and justify the categories if needed.
   c. Ask students to work in pairs or individually to choose a category of terms about which to write a brief paragraph. It may be necessary to model the composition of one or more paragraphs with the whole class before releasing the responsibility to the students. Encourage them to use the displayed terms and refer to the reading selection when necessary.

Example: World History: European Middle Ages: Feudalism

TOPIC—MIDDLE AGES: FEUDALISM

Brainstorming (whole class)

feudalism	chivalry	knights
manor	religion	royalty
lord	serf	Middle Ages
kingdom		

Grouping and labeling (small groups)

Concepts & Ideas	Places	People	Time Periods
feudalism	castle	lord	Middle Ages
chivalry	kingdom	kings	
religion		knights	
royalty			

Post-reading: Adding new terms (whole class or small groups)

secular	vassal	manor
peasants	fief	clergy
serfs	tithe	

Grouping and labeling new terms with old terms (small groups)

Concepts & Systems	Places	People/ and Roles		Time Periods	Things "Given"
feudalism	castle	lord	*vassal*	Middle Ages	*tithe*
chivalry	kingdom	kings	*peasants*		*fief*
religion	*manor*	knights			
royalty		*serfs*			
secular		*clergy*			

Writing Exercise (pairs or individuals). The structure of feudalism is like a pyramid of distinct roles and classes. At the top of the pyramid, with the most power, is the king. Next are the wealthy lords or landowners and high-ranking clergy such as bishops. At the next level of power are the knights—warriors on horseback who defend their lords' land in exchange for fiefs or land. At the bottom of the pyramid are the landless peasants or serfs who work the land for their lords.

Variations
- List-Group-Label and Write can be used in whole class situations, collaborative learning groups, pairs, or by individuals.
- Advanced students may use this strategy independently while reading other passages or chapters in their textbooks.
- Students can be asked to answer a writing prompt using as many of the words in their responses as possible.

$\bigcirc$ **S-2**

THE PRE-READING PLAN (PreP)

PreP, created by Langer (1981), has two main segments. The first portion is class discussion and the second involves analyzing student responses. It has the following objectives:

- To give students an opportunity to generate what they know about a topic.
- To encourage students to extend their generated ideas.
- To show students how to evaluate their ideas.
- To provide teachers with a method for assessing the adequacy of students' prior knowledge about a specific topic.
- To determine the language students use to express their ideas.

Materials
Selected text passage, chapters, or
a combination of multiple sources

Content Areas
All

Procedure
1. Choose a topic to study; then select a passage or chapter to be read by students.
2. Prior to starting the class discussion, determine key concepts for students to address and in which ways the discussion may be prompted and stimulated.
3. Introduce the topic to students with a picture, film, quotation, or interesting artifact.
4. Initial Associations with the Concept. Using the picture or other stimuli, ask the students to brainstorm: *What comes to mind when…? What do you think of…? What might you see, hear, feel…? What might be going on…? etc.* As students verbalize their ideas, write them on the board or overhead transparency.
5. Reflections on Initial Associations. Ask the students to explain the free associations they generated in the previous step. Encourage them to become aware of the basis of their own associations, as well as their peers' ideas. Encourage the students to evaluate the usefulness of these ideas. *What made you think of…? How is this idea connected…?*
6. Reformulation of Knowledge. Ask students if they have any new ideas or if they want to change any of the existing ideas. Encourage them to revise, delete, or add to the brainstormed ideas. Do not evaluate; instead, be accepting and inquisitive.

7. Analyzing student responses. Determine if students have well-formed, partly formed, or ill-formed knowledge structures.

    a. Students with little understanding of a concept will generally focus on low-level associations with morphemes (prefixes, suffixes, or root words)— words that sound like the stimulus word, or words that are similar but not quite relevant.

    b. Students with some prior information will generally mention examples, attributes, or defining characteristics.

    c. Students with much prior understanding of a concept will generally offer information that suggests evidence of integration with high-level concepts. Their responses might take the form of analogies, definitions, linkages, or superordinate concepts.

Example: Biology—Mammals and Their Characteristics

DIAGNOSTIC ANALYSIS OF STUDENT RESPONSES TO PreP

GENERAL TOPIC: Mammals

KEY TOPIC: Characteristics of Mammals. (pictures of various mammals)

Student	Responses	Level
Megan	1. no eggs	some-attribute
	2. mammals have hair	
	3. dogs, cats, horses	little-association
Bill	1. they are intelligent and must be able to perform complex behaviors	much-superordinate
	2. limbs, legs	some - attribute
	3. diaphragms for breathing	
Eric	1. mammals nurse their babies, but reptiles do not	much-analogies
	2. mammals can keep a constant body temperature so they can survive in extreme climates	much-superodinate
	3. mammals have different ways to gather food	some-attribute
Latiesha	1. jungle animals, pets	little-association
	2. weird mammals – bats, porcupines	
	3. some mammals have camouflage	some-attribute

Variations

- The associations generated during PreP may be used to extend the lesson *after* reading. Students may delete, add, or make changes to their ideas created during the pre-reading stage.
- The generated associations may also serve as writing starters or prompts in the post-reading stage.
- Students may edit or revise associations in pairs or small groups following the whole class discussion.

S-3

WORD SORTS

Word Sorts (Readence, Moore, & Rickelman, 2000) is a technique used to organize words from a reading selection. Two types of word sorts, closed and open, are used for categorizing words. When using closed word sorts, the teacher chooses 10-15 words from a reading selection and provides categories for the words. Students discuss the words and place each under the appropriate category. (The words and categories can be written on slips of paper so they can be moved around). Next, students discuss reasons for their categorization. After the selection is read, students can revise their categories.

When using open word sorts, the teacher chooses 10-15 words from a reading selection and the students discuss each word. Students then develop their own categories and place each word under the appropriate heading, giving reasons for their choices. After the selection is read, students can revise their categories.

Materials
List of targeted words

Content Areas
All

Procedure

1. Using the closed or open sort process, give students a list of words to categorize. This list can include words that are or are not used in the selection they will read.
2. Give students slips of paper (or have them make their own) to write the words on so that they can move them around.
3. In order to categorize the words, students will use categories, such as *can define*, *have seen or heard*, and *don't know*. Depending on what is being read and the content area, the categories may be changed and decided upon by the teacher or students.
4. In groups, students will discuss the reasons for their organization.
5. After reading the passage, students will revise their categories as they see fit.

Example: Sample Music Word Sort Lesson

SAMPLE MUSIC WORD SORT LESSON

1. Give students the following list of words as an introduction to terms associated with music:

key	meter	rhythm
melody	pattern	treble clef
bass clef	pitch	dynamics
tempo	articulation	melodic patterns
cues	harmony	instrument

2. Have students make strips of paper on which they will write one word.

3. Identify the categories they will use, such as
   can define   have seen/heard   don't know

4. Divide students into groups to discuss their reasons for organizing the words the way they did and get feedback from each other.

5. Encourage students to make their organization choices orally to make a master chart. The teacher defines each word so students will be familiar with the terms.

Variations

- When used with other subject areas, categories such as the following can be used:

Words with prefixes	Words with one or two syllables
Words you think are interesting	Words that are nouns
Words that aren't so interesting	Words with two or more syllables

- This strategy could be used to introduce a passage as well as to review vocabulary words.
- This strategy also works well with content-specific categories, such as classifying Civil War terms as referring to either the North, the South, or both.
- The example given is a closed word sort. When using the open word sort strategy, the teacher provides the words while the students come up with appropriate categories in groups or as a class.

$$S-4$$

SEMANTIC FEATURE ANALYSIS GRID

Semantic Feature Analysis is a strategy that provides students with opportunities to discuss the features of words and thus acquire deeper levels of understanding of them. Specifically, Semantic Feature Analysis assists students' understanding of the relationships between words or terms that are semantically connected and have similarities and differences based on identified features. The features are characteristics of the words that are shared. This strategy provides the students with a way to organize words in a relationship grid (Johnson & Pearson, 1984). A grid is constructed that has the semantically related words down the left column and features that they have in common listed across the top. At the intersection of the words and features on the grid, the students discuss whether to put a plus or minus to indicate that the particular word does or does not reflect that feature. This activity can be done in large group settings as the teacher leads the discussion. After the students have an understanding of the process, they can do this activity in small groups or pairs. An important point is that it should not be done alone since discussion is a critical component of the activity.

Materials
Text containing words that share common features; a Semantic Feature Analysis Grid worksheet

Content Areas
All

Procedure

1. Identify a topic to be analyzed and then select a list of semantically connected vocabulary words that share common features.
2. Design a grid to show the lists of words down the left column and the features that are shared among the words across the top. It is helpful to save time during the activity if the chart lists the words in order as they appear in the text. Also, at this time, you might need to clarify some specific parts of the terms. For example, in the following sample about taxes, the teacher has to define the word "estate" in the term "estate tax" since many students perceived the term to mean "a state tax."
3. Now lead students in a discussion of whether a plus or a minus (or yes/no) should be placed in the intersection of the word and the feature. Group consensus determines the symbol placed in the cell. The process of discussing whether the word does or does not possess that feature is a valuable component of this activity.

4. After the pluses and minuses have been placed in all cells, have students look for patterns or common features of words. You can prompt with such questions as "Do all of the words share more than one feature?" or "Do you see patterns with some words sharing certain features and not others?"

LESSON: AMERICAN GOVERNMENT—FEDERAL TAXES

1. *Prereading Stage:* Select terms to be analyzed, identify features, and place them in a grid. Students place pluses or minuses in the chart based on group consensus before reading the text on federal taxes.

SEMANTIC FEATURE ANALYSIS GRID

	Features of Taxes			
Types of Taxes	the greater the ability to pay, the higher the percentage or rate of money collected	allows for exemptions and/or reductions	taxes are levied at a fixed rate	a major source of income for the federal government
income tax				
individual income tax				
payroll tax				
social insurance tax				
unemployment tax				
gift tax				
luxury tax				
progressive tax				
corporate income tax				
regressive tax				
excise tax				
estate tax				
custom tax (tariff, import duty, impost)				

2. *Reading Stage:* Direct students to work in groups to determine their responses to the pluses and minuses in the grid. They may change the symbols as they read the text for clarification and understanding.

3. *Post-Reading Stage:* Conduct a class discussion about student responses and make necessary changes.

PARTIAL STUDENT SAMPLE OF SEMANTIC FEATURE ANALYSIS GRID ON TAXES

	Features of Taxes			
Types of Taxes	the greater the ability to pay, the higher the percentage or rate of money collected	allows for exemptions and/or reductions	taxes are levied at a fixed rate	a major source of income for the federal government
income tax	?	Yes	?	Yes
individual income tax	Yes	Yes	No	Yes
payroll tax	No	No		
social insurance tax	No	No	Yes	No
unemployment tax	No	No	Yes	No
gift tax	No	Yes	Yes	No
luxury tax	?	Yes	Yes	No

Variations

- Create a Semantic Feature Analysis Grid; supply all the semantically related words in the grid as well as the features associated with them. Then direct students to fill in the grid with pluses or minuses as they discuss whether each word does or does not possess this feature. This can be done before the reading to assess the background knowledge of the group and be revisited after the reading. It can also be done after independent reading to help students organize their understanding of what they have read.

- Do the same as above, but allow students to fill in the grid as they encounter the words in the text. This can be done as students work in groups during the reading.

- Elicit a more complex level of student involvement by supplying a partially developed grid that lists the features and a few of the words. Then students use the text to complete the list of words.

- An alternate and more difficult activity is to supply the list of words and one feature as a model and then guide the students in a discussion where they supply the rest of the features, completing the grid with pluses and minuses. As students encounter words with unique features, these additional features can be added, and the other words already completed can be revisited to fill in the plus or minus for that feature.

(Blackline Master)

SEMANTIC FEATURE ANALYSIS GRID

Terms	Features									

Instructional Strategies for Teaching Content Vocabulary, Grades 4-12, by Janis M. Harmon, Karen D. Wood, and Wanda B. Hedrick. Published by National Middle School Association and International Reading Association. Copyright 2006 by National Middle School Association.

S-5

VOCAB-O-GRAM

The Vocab-O-Gram (Blachowicz & Fisher, 2002) is a visual organizer for
- Helping students organize new and familiar terms.
- Providing a structure to aid students in making predictions about words and phrases.
- Enabling students to manipulate words by considering their relationships to other words and concepts.
- Providing a springboard for pre- and post-reading discussions.

Materials
Vocab-O-Gram chart (see blackline master)
Text passage to read during class

Content Area
Social Studies

Procedure

1. Select a text passage for students to read in class. Read the passage carefully to determine categories for the Vocab-O-Gram. Then reread to find words and phrases that match the categories. Some words and phrases may work under multiple categories. To support English Language Learners, be mindful of selecting terms that may have multiple meanings. Clarify the meaning that is intended for the text passage.

2. Develop a two-column category chart with your category headings in the first column and corresponding prompts in the second column. Refer to the following example for suggestions about the prompts.

3. Introduce the passage to students. Explain the purpose of the Vocab-O-Gram by telling students that making predictions is an important process in comprehending texts. This will enable them to set expectations for reading.

4. Have students work in small groups to complete the category chart. Allow 15 to 20 minutes for this section. Use small, heterogeneous groups to make initial predictions that will support English Language Learners. Students in the group can clarify any unfamiliar terms.

5. Once groups have completed the Vocab-O-Gram, bring the class together to discuss group responses. Ask a spokesperson from each group to provide a rationale for why the group classified specific words and phrases under a particular heading.

6. Then direct students to read the passage silently to verify their responses. English Language Learners may read with a partner.

7. After reading, discuss any changes students make, and ask them to support these moves.

Example: Topic—*Trial By Ice: A Photobiography of Sir Ernest Shackleton* by K.M. Kostyal, pp. 9-23.

Predict how the author might use the following words:

National Antarctic Expedition	rivalry	driving blizzards
Antarctica	squawking penguins	world's last frontier
travel by horse and buggy	March 1901	unseen crevasses
roaring sea	adventure	scurvy
ice floes	merchant marine	whiteouts
humiliation	no sunshine	pemmican
good natured	seal meat	blowing hiss of whales
expedition	rookeries	hungry, cold, and exhausted
pack ice	hoosh	latitude 82° 17'
solitude	glacial ice and snow	
Southern Hemisphere	Ross Ice Shelf	

Environment ice floes roaring sea blowing hiss of whales squawking penguins	*What would the environment be like?* Cold, wet, and dangerous
People good natured solitude adventure merchant marine	*What can you tell about Shackleton?* Nice man who maybe likes to be by himself
Event expedition National Antarctic Expedition	*What ideas do you have about these events?* It takes a lot of people to go on an expedition.
Time travel by horse and buggy March 1901	*What ideas do you have about this time period?* This happened a long time ago before people used cars and planes.
Place Antarctica world's last frontier Southern Hemisphere Ross Ice Shelf	*What ideas do you have about these places?* Very cold

Problem glacial ice and snow pack ice driving blizzards unseen crevasses rivalry no sunshine scurvy whiteouts hungry, cold, and exhausted	*What ideas do you have about the problem(s)?* Shackleton had to live through terrible winter weather.
Solution seal meat latitude 82° 17'	*What ideas do you have about the solution?* They didn't have enough food so they ate seal meat.
Impact humiliation	*Make a prediction about the impact of these events.* Shackleton did not make it to the South Pole so he was embarrassed.

Questions you may have
  Why did Shackleton want to go to the
  South Pole?	

Unfamiliar words or phrases rookeries hoosh pemmican	

Variations

- Challenge interested students to create the categories and words for another passage.
- Develop a writing prompt, and ask students to use some of the words and phrases in their responses.
- Create a game board with the categories, and write the words and phrases on strips of paper. Students in each group must place a word or phrase under a category. Consider laminating the board and paper strips.

(SOCIAL STUDIES CATEGORIES)

Predict how the author might use the following words:	

Environment	**What would the environment be like?**
People	**What can you tell about the people?**
Event	**What ideas do you have about these events?**
Time	**What ideas do you have about this time period?**
Place	**What ideas do you have about these places?**
Problem	**What ideas do you have about the problem(s)?**
Solution	**What ideas do you have about the solution?**
Impact	**Make a prediction about the impact of these events.**
Questions you may have	
Unfamiliar words or phrases	

Adapted from Blachowicz, C., & Fisher, P.J. (2006). *Teaching vocabulary in all classrooms* (3rd ed.). Upper Saddle River, NJ: Pearson Merrill Prentice Hall.

S-6

ZOOMING IN AND ZOOMING OUT

Zooming In and Zooming Out (Harmon & Hedrick, 2000) is an instructional framework for assisting teachers in introducing and reinforcing the meaning of conceptually important terms in a specific content area, and guiding class discussions and reading about an important term that is critical for understanding the topic at hand.

There are three important parts of this strategy:

1. Zooming In: Students closely examine a concept by rank ordering important information and by discussing unrelated or improbable ideas.
2. Zooming Out: Students situate the concept within a larger picture by discussing similar or parallel concepts and discussing related concepts, ideas, or events.
3. Summarizing: Students write a statement that synthesizes what they have learned about the concept.

Materials

Three sheets of chart paper for *brainstorming, fact-finding,* and *visual display*

Texts

Fact-finding sheet

Content Areas

All

Procedure

1. Select a term that is conceptually important for understanding the chapter. Place the term in the center of one sheet of chart paper. Lead the students in brainstorming what they already know about the topic.
2. Assign readings about the topic. Try to provide materials from multiple sources such as library books, an encyclopedia, or the Internet. This will be especially helpful for struggling readers and English Language Learners. Allow students to work in groups as they search for facts while they read. In this way, students with special needs can elicit the help of peers.
3. Ask groups to share facts they found in reading. Write this new information on the second sheet of chart paper, adding to the previously generated list. Cross out any unsubstantiated or misconstrued information from the brainstorming list.
4. Most important and least important information. Have students take the information supplied in Step 1 and Step 2 and prioritize it from most important to least. Have the students vote for the top three and rank order the list based on the number of votes. Place the results of most important and least important information on the last chart paper, which is the beginning of the visual display.

5. Unrelated ideas, events, or people. Ask students to identify ideas, places, or events not associated with the topic. A prompt can be, "What are some things you would not expect ___ to do?" Write student responses on the visual display.

6. Similar to. Ask students to identify ideas, people, or places that are similar to the topic. For example, if the topic is a place, the student could identify a similar place. Write the suggestions on the visual display. A prompt can be, "What does this remind you of?" Write student responses on the visual display.

7. Related ideas, events, or people. Ask students to identify ideas, places, or events related to the topic. For example, if the topic is a person, students could suggest events or ideas that are related. A prompt can be, "You cannot talk about _____ without talking about _____." Place them on the display.

8. Summary statement. Ask students to summarize the activity by providing a short wrap-up of the topic. For example, you might say, "If you had to say something about this idea in six words or less, what would it be?" You could also use the clue words "Somebody Wanted But So."

Examples: See the following pages for *Harriet Tubman* and *artifacts*.

Variations

- Zooming In and Zooming Out also works well as a review activity to reinforce conceptual learning before students take a test.

Blackline Master

The blackline master provides a practice sheet for teachers. We strongly recommend that after teachers select a term, they complete the practice sheet first to anticipate the types of responses that each category may elicit for that particular term.

ZOOMING OUT...

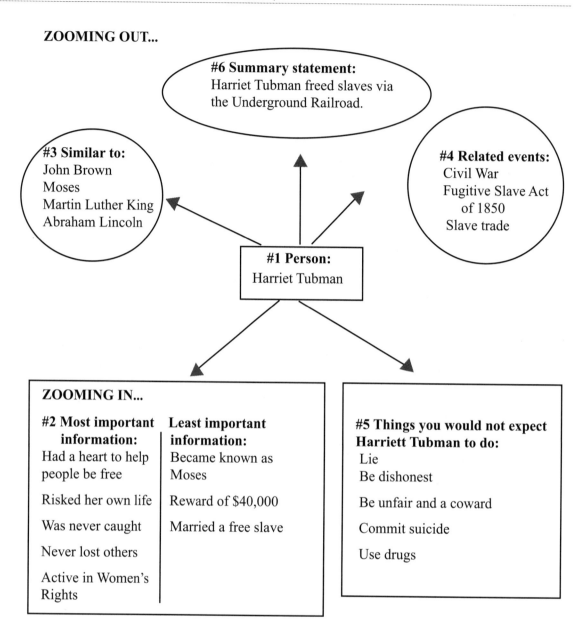

#6 Summary statement:
Harriet Tubman freed slaves via the Underground Railroad.

#3 Similar to:
John Brown
Moses
Martin Luther King
Abraham Lincoln

#4 Related events:
Civil War
Fugitive Slave Act
of 1850
Slave trade

#1 Person:
Harriet Tubman

ZOOMING IN...

#2 Most important information:	**Least important information:**
Had a heart to help people be free	Became known as Moses
Risked her own life	Reward of $40,000
Was never caught	Married a free slave
Never lost others	
Active in Women's Rights	

#5 Things you would not expect Harriett Tubman to do:
Lie
Be dishonest

Be unfair and a coward

Commit suicide

Use drugs

Source: Harmon, J. M., & Hedrick, W. B. (2000). Zooming in and zooming out: Enhancing vocabulary and conceptual learning in social studies. *The Reading Teacher, 54*(2), 155-159. Copyright 2000 by the International Reading Association. All rights reserved. Used by permission of the International Reading Association.

ZOOMING OUT...

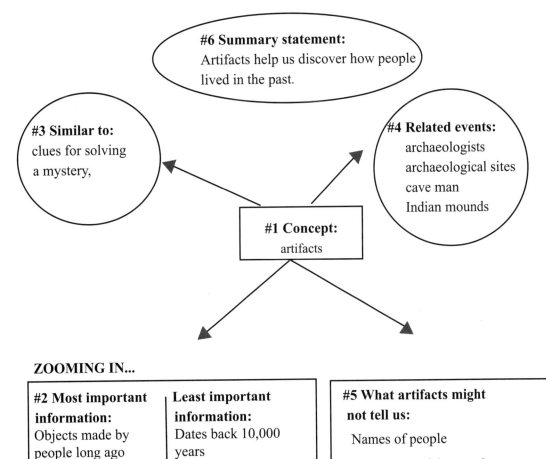

ZOOMING IN...

#2 Most important information:	**Least important information:**	**#5 What artifacts might not tell us:**
Objects made by people long ago	Dates back 10,000 years	Names of people
Tells how people lived	Pottery, jewelry, tools	Personality of the people
Indian mounds used in burial and religious ceremonies	Prehistory means before history	Physical appearance of the people
		Size of families

Source: Harmon, J. M., & Hedrick, W. B. (2000). Zooming in and zooming out: Enhancing vocabulary and conceptual learning in social studies. *The Reading Teacher, 54*(2), 155-159. Copyright 2000 by the International Reading Association. All rights reserved. Used by permission of the International Reading Association.

ZOOMING IN

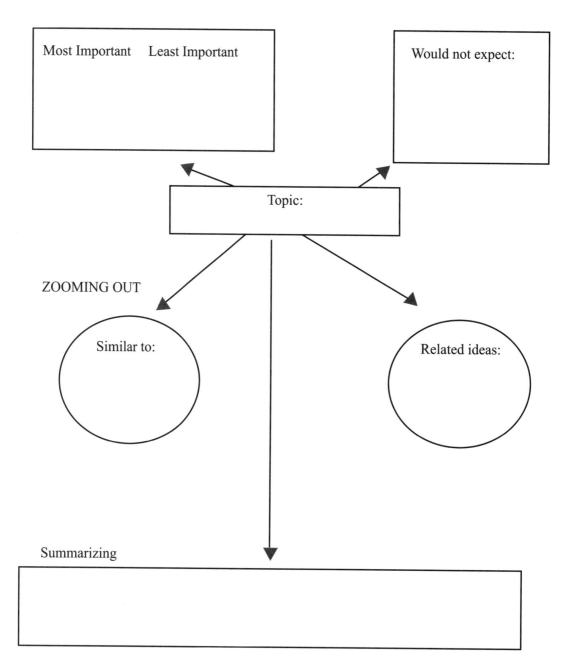

Most Important   Least Important

Would not expect:

Topic:

ZOOMING OUT

Similar to:

Related ideas:

Summarizing

Source: Harmon, J. M., & Hedrick, W. B. (2000). Zooming in and zooming out: Enhancing vocabulary and conceptual learning in social studies. *The Reading Teacher*, *54*(2), 155-159. Copyright 2000 by the International Reading Association. All rights reserved. Used by permission of the International Reading Association

$$\boxed{S\text{-}7}$$

GRAPHIC ORGANIZERS

Graphic Organizers are visual representations that show both spatial and hierarchal relationships among ideas and concepts. They can be used to represent processes, indicate a sequence of events, show inner relationships among concepts, or categorize and classify information. Research studies on graphic organizers have provided the following information:

- Graphic organizers work well as a prereading activity to help students link information to what they already know (Merkley & Jefferies, 2000/2001).
- Graphic organizers increase comprehension when students construct them during reading and after reading activities (Alvermann & Boothby, 1986; cited in Merkley & Jefferies, 2000/2001).
- Graphic organizers enhance learning when they are used with other strategies, such as summarizing and retelling (Bean, Singer, Sorter, & Frasee, 1986).

Graphic organizers are versatile teaching tools that help students understand many concepts across different content areas as well as support the literacy tasks they confront in content area classrooms.

Content Areas
All

History Example: Requires transparency for overhead and copies of a chosen graphic organizer.

Procedure for Using Graphic Organizers as a Prereading Activity

1. Develop a graphic organizer that can serve as an overview of a passage students will read. The example below represents a visual display for information in Chapter Four of *The Boys' War* by Jim Murphy. This chapter discusses the duties and problems faced by drummer boys during the Civil War. Include important terms (e.g., *disillusioned, muster*) that students will encounter while reading.
2. Using a transparency of the graphic organizer, discuss each segment of the organizer telling students to pay attention to these topics when they read the chapter. For example, begin by telling the students, "Looking at the graphic organizer, this chapter entitled 'Drumbeats and Bullets' will discuss drummer boys. You will read about what it was like to be a drummer boy. Remember how the boys were so anxious and excited to go to war. But you will find in this chapter that the boys soon became *disappointed* and *disillusioned*. In other words, their expectations of fun and excitement were dashed. You become *disillusioned* when you expect something wonderful and then find out

differently. Pay attention to what made the boys feel this way and then write it in the circles under these terms." Continue the discussion in this manner for the whole organizer.

3. As students read the chapter, direct them to complete the graphic organizer. During this time, offer individual assistance to clarify instructions for students who may need modifications. Some students may benefit from working in pairs to read and complete the graphic organizer.

4. After reading, discuss student answers. Have students volunteer to write their answers on the transparency.

5. Direct students to use the information from the graphic organizer to write a brief summary of the information in the space at the bottom of the graphic organizer. Encourage them to use the following terms in their summary: *disillusioned*, *drummer boy*, and *muster*.

(adapted from Merkley & Jefferies, 2000/2001)

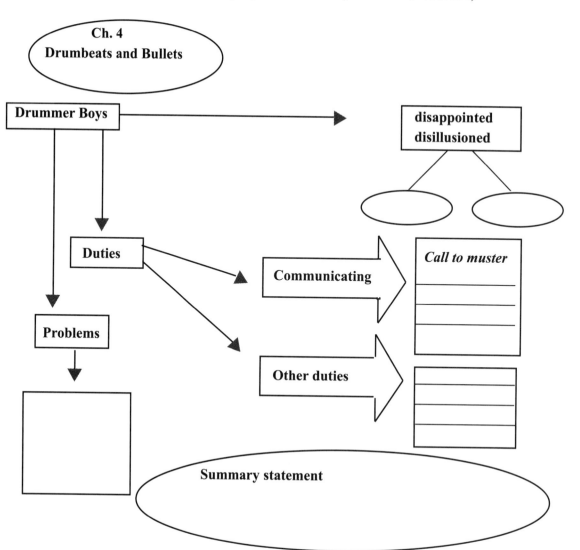

Mathematics Example: Requires transparency for overhead and copies of a chosen graphic organizer.

Procedure for Using Graphic Organizers as a Prereading Activity

(adapted from Merkley & Jefferies, 2000/2001):

1. Develop a graphic organizer that will highlight the important terminology discussed in the text students will be reading. In this example, students will be reading about different kinds of polygons.
2. Show a transparency of the graphic organizer and provide copies for students.
3. Begin by providing a definition of a polygon. "A polygon is a closed geometric figure with sides made up of line segments." Write this definition on the graphic organizer and ask students to do the same on their copy.
4. Urge students to pay attention as they read about what is and what is not a polygon.
   Direct them to draw a figure that is a polygon and a figure that is not a polygon in the appropriate boxes.
5. Continue to discuss the other sections of the graphic organizer, pointing out the specific information that students need to find to complete the graphic organizer.

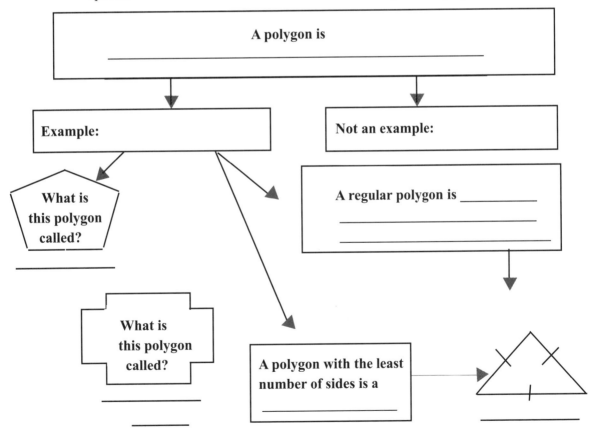

History Example: Requires text passage and paper

Procedure for Using Graphic Organizers During and After Reading

1. Provide students with a list of important terms they will encounter in reading and can use for their graphic organizer. The first example is a passage about art and artists of the Holocaust. The terms for students to use follow:

Holocaust	concentration camps	propaganda
official art	illegal	Terezin
unofficial art	Jews	Nazi party

2. Discuss the words with the students as a pre-reading activity. Ask students such questions as the following:
   - Do you recognize any of the words? What do you know about the words?
   - Which words are proper names of events, places, or people? How do you know? Can you tell if it is a person, event, or place?
   - Point out prefixes in *illegal* and *unofficial art*. Remind students that these prefixes mean *not*.
   - Discuss the meaning of the words, pointing out that *official art* and *unofficial art* mean the opposite. Tell students that these two terms could be the focal point of a graphic organizer.
3. Work together with the students to begin a rough representation of a graphic organizer using *official art* and *unofficial art* as a starting point. Tell students to pay attention to ideas that are connected to these two terms.
4. Direct students to read the passage. To support diverse learners the teacher can read it orally, or students can read to each other in pairs.
5. Ask students to complete a graphic organizer to represent the concepts presented and to use the words listed above.
6. Remind students that they can use the graphic organizer to retell the main points and to use as a study guide when preparing for a test.

Two examples of graphic organizers follow, one from social studies and one from biology.

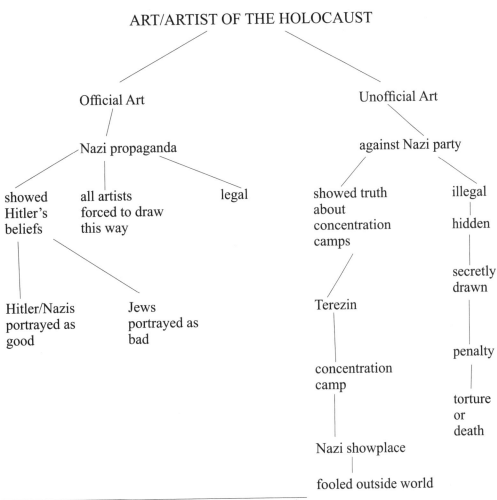

ART/ARTIST OF THE HOLOCAUST

Official Art

Nazi propaganda

showed Hitler's beliefs

all artists forced to draw this way

legal

Hitler/Nazis portrayed as good

Jews portrayed as bad

Unofficial Art

against Nazi party

showed truth about concentration camps

illegal

hidden

secretly drawn

Terezin

concentration camp

penalty

torture or death

Nazi showplace

fooled outside world

Special thanks to Mitzi Sprado for contributing this example.

Biology Example: Text passage and paper needed

Procedure for Using Graphic Organizers During and After Reading

1. Provide students with a list of important terms they will encounter in their reading and can use for their graphic organizer. This example is a passage describing the parts of the eye. Important terms include the following:

sclera	iris	pupil	cornea	lens muscle
rod	cone	optic nerve	retina	vitreous humor

2. Discuss the words with students as a prereading activity. Ask such questions as:
    *   Do you recognize any of the words? What do you know about the words?
    *   Point out that *optos* is the Greek root for *visible*. Discuss related terms, such as *optometrist*, *ophthalmologist*.

3. Work together with the students to begin a rough representation of a graphic organizer using the following major categories: *outer parts of the eye* and *inner parts of the eye*.

4. Direct students to read the passage. Reading options to support diverse learners include: the teacher can read it orally, or students can read to each other in pairs.

5. Ask students to complete a graphic organizer to represent the concepts presented, and use the words listed above.

6. Remind students that they can use the graphic organizer to retell the main points and use as a study guide when preparing for an exam.

7. An example follows:

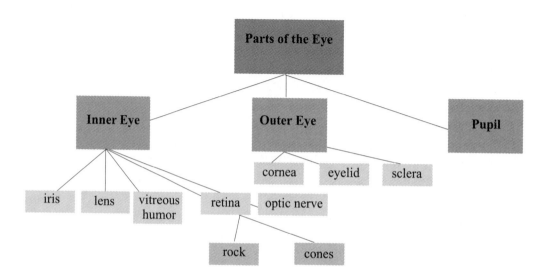

Variations

- Students can work with a partner or independently to create study guides for a unit of study.
- Display a variety of graphic organizers and allow student choice for differentiating a product for a content area assignment.
- Using the internet, classroom resources, and the library, allow students to use graphic organizers as a tool to gather notes for a research assignment.

S-8

CONCEPT OF DEFINITION MAP

A Concept of Definition Map provides a framework for helping students consider important features of a term (Schwartz & Raphael, 1985; Schwartz, 1988). These features include

- Category (What is it?)
- Properties (What is it like?)
- Illustrations (What are some examples?)

The mapping can also be extended to address such questions as "What is the purpose?" or "How do you do this?" The goal is to support students as they internalize the features to help them define and learn concepts. The mapping works well with nouns rather than verbs. The Concept of Definition map can be used as an introduction to a new concept and as a tool for review and reinforcement.

Materials
Blank map

Content Areas
Social Studies
Mathematics
Science

Procedure

1. Discuss with students what it means to define words. Explain that concepts can be defined by their features, such as category, properties, and examples.
2. Introduce the Concept of Definition Map using one of the examples provided here. Use pictures or other visuals as part of the mapping.
3. As a whole class, work together to create a Concept of Definition Map for a familiar term.
4. Have students work in groups to develop their own Concept of Definition Map for concepts that are highlighted in the current lesson.

Examples

Scientific notation
Endocrine system
Geographic regions

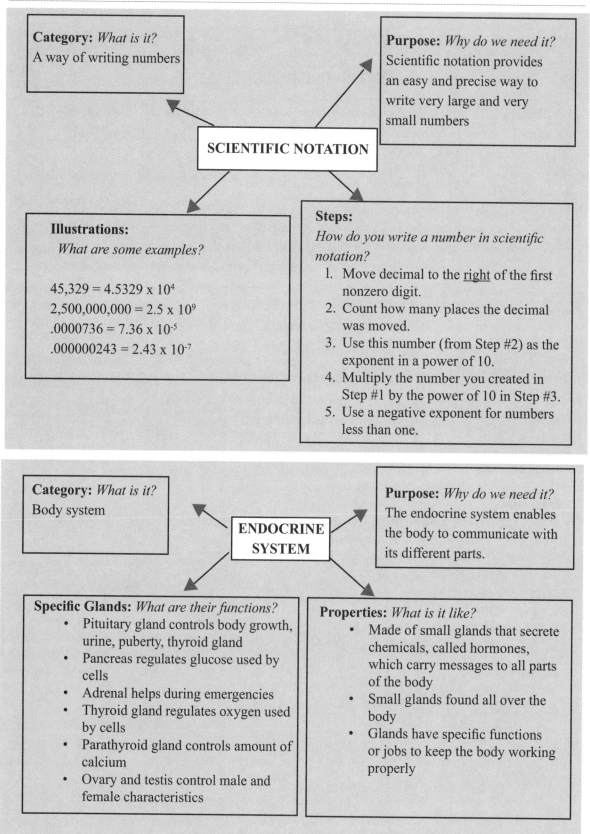

Category: *What is it?*
A way of writing numbers

Purpose: *Why do we need it?*
Scientific notation provides an easy and precise way to write very large and very small numbers

SCIENTIFIC NOTATION

Illustrations:
What are some examples?

$45,329 = 4.5329 \times 10^4$
$2,500,000,000 = 2.5 \times 10^9$
$.0000736 = 7.36 \times 10^{-5}$
$.000000243 = 2.43 \times 10^{-7}$

Steps:
How do you write a number in scientific notation?
1. Move decimal to the <u>right</u> of the first nonzero digit.
2. Count how many places the decimal was moved.
3. Use this number (from Step #2) as the exponent in a power of 10.
4. Multiply the number you created in Step #1 by the power of 10 in Step #3.
5. Use a negative exponent for numbers less than one.

Category: *What is it?*
Body system

ENDOCRINE SYSTEM

Purpose: *Why do we need it?*
The endocrine system enables the body to communicate with its different parts.

Specific Glands: *What are their functions?*
- Pituitary gland controls body growth, urine, puberty, thyroid gland
- Pancreas regulates glucose used by cells
- Adrenal helps during emergencies
- Thyroid gland regulates oxygen used by cells
- Parathyroid gland controls amount of calcium
- Ovary and testis control male and female characteristics

Properties: *What is it like?*
- Made of small glands that secrete chemicals, called hormones, which carry messages to all parts of the body
- Small glands found all over the body
- Glands have specific functions or jobs to keep the body working properly

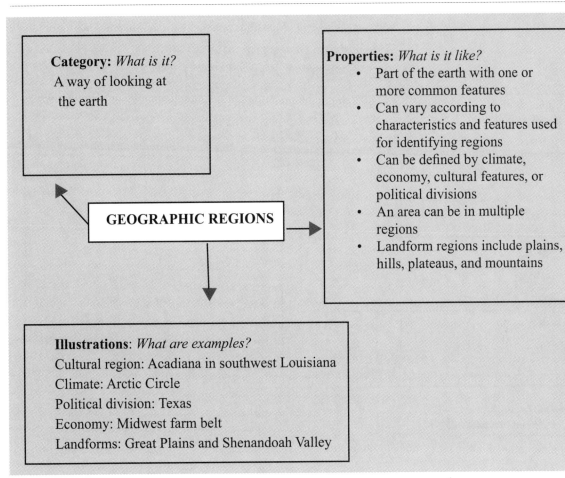

Category: *What is it?*
A way of looking at
the earth

Properties: *What is it like?*
- Part of the earth with one or
  more common features
- Can vary according to
  characteristics and features used
  for identifying regions
- Can be defined by climate,
  economy, cultural features, or
  political divisions
- An area can be in multiple
  regions
- Landform regions include plains,
  hills, plateaus, and mountains

GEOGRAPHIC REGIONS

Illustrations: *What are examples?*
Cultural region: Acadiana in southwest Louisiana
Climate: Arctic Circle
Political division: Texas
Economy: Midwest farm belt
Landforms: Great Plains and Shenandoah Valley

Variations

- Use other categories that may help students understand a term. For example, in
  the scientific notation example, the category "Purpose" reminds students of the
  importance of scientific notation. The category "Steps" enables students to review the
  procedure for changing numbers to scientific notation.
- Have students create Concept of Definition Maps to teach terms to the
  rest of the class.

(Blackline Master)

CONCEPT OF DEFINITION MAP
(Source: Schwartz & Raphael, 1985)

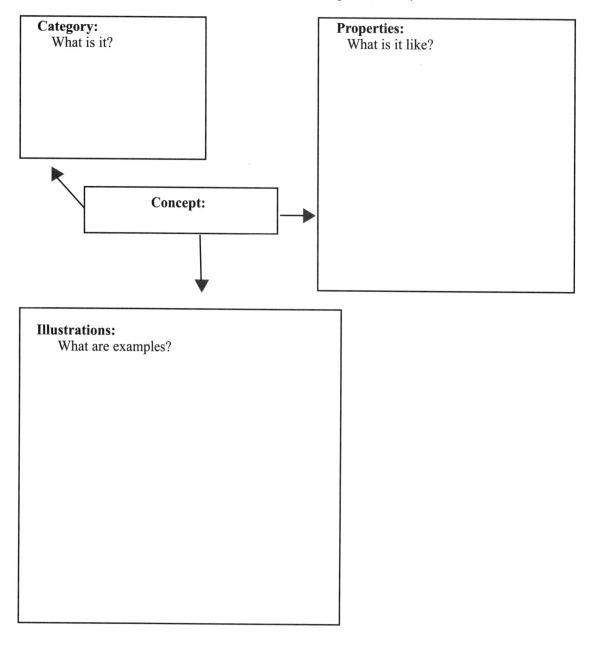

Category:
 What is it?

Properties:
 What is it like?

Concept:

Illustrations:
 What are examples?

Instructional Strategies for Teaching Content Vocabulary, Grades 4-12, by Janis M. Harmon, Karen D. Wood, and Wanda B. Hedrick. Published by National Middle School Association and International Reading Association. Copyright 2006 by National Middle School Association.

S-9

WORD ANALOGIES

Analogies are useful tools for bridging known concepts to new and familiar concepts. They enable students to see the relationship or similarity between words and ideas, to engage in critical thinking and reasoning tasks, and to be creative and divergent thinkers. Analogies require students to make inferences as they internalize specific features about a concept. Content teachers should be mindful of students' background knowledge and experiences to avoid comparisons that may confuse students, especially those who are learning English as a second language.

Materials:
Analogy examples;
Think sheet for using analogies

Content Areas
All

Procedure

1. Begin by discussing the format of analogies. Explain the symbols used with analogies:

    : refers to the words "is to"

    :: refers to the word "as"

2. Tell students that because words can have different relationships with other words, there are different types of analogies, such as the following:

    part to whole (finger : hand :: toe : foot)

    person to situation (Roosevelt : Great Depression :: Lincoln : Civil War)

    cause and effect (aging : facial wrinkles :: sunbathing : tan

    synonym (master : expert :: novice : apprentice)

    antonym (naive : sophisticated :: alien : native)

    geography (Rocky Mountains : west :: Appalachian Mountains : east)

    measurement (inches : ruler :: minutes : clock)

    examples (Folgers : Maxwell House :: Cheerios : Corn Flakes)

    functions (switch : lamp :: key : door)

3. Using the examples above, model the thinking processes needed to understand analogies.

4. Explain to students that analogies can be used to help understand new concepts in a particular subject matter area, such as science.

5. Present examples of analogies for the lesson topic. For the first example, model the relationship between the terms by thinking out loud. Then, ask for a volunteer to think aloud for the next example.

Example: Computers

COMPUTER ANALOGIES

Directions: For each analogy, do the following: state the relationship, provide a reasonable term, and justify your answer.

ignite **:** fire **::** _____ **:** computer (action done to an object)
    Relationship: _action done to an object_
    Term: **boot**
    Justification: _You start a fire by igniting it and you start a computer by booting it up._

jam **:** lock **:: freeze :** computer (action done to an object)
    Relationship: _____
    Term: _____
    Justification: _____

word **:** sentence **:: byte :** computer information (part to whole)
    Relationship: _____
    Term: _____
    Justification: _____

letter **:** word **:: bit :** byte (part to whole)
    Relationship: _____
    Term: _____
    Justification: _____

vertical **:** horizontal **:: portrait:** landscape (antonyms)
    Relationship: _____
    Term: _____
    Justification: _____

Ford **:** Honda **:: PC :** Mac (examples of different types)
    Relationship: _____
    Term: _____
    Justification: _____

181 Black Oak Drive **:** Harmon address **:: URL :** computer address
    Relationship: _____
    Term: _____
    Justification: _____

filing cabinet **:** office **:: database :** computer (function)
    Relationship: _____
    Term: _____
    Justification: _____

burglar alarm **:** home **:: firewall :** computer (function)
    Relationship: _____
    Term: _____
    Justification: _____

thief **:** bank **:: hacker :** computer program (person to place)
    Relationship: _____
    Term: _____
    Justification: _____

Refer to the following Web links for other examples of analogies related to computers and technology:

http://www.nsta.org/main/news/stories/college_science.php?news_story_ID=47561
http://www.gustavus.lib.ak.us/computer/training/lesson1.htm

Variations

- Have students work in groups to discuss possible terms for each analogy. Students must support their thinking by providing a legitimate rationale for their choice of terms.
- Ask students to create their own analogies.

S-10

FORCED ASSOCIATIONS

Forced Associations is a vocabulary activity that bolsters both comprehension and creativity (Middleton, 1991). For this exercise, students are asked to make a connection between two obviously different terms. The teacher may select random dictionary words for students to associate with specific content vocabulary terms that have been recently studied. Another possibility is to ask students to make associations between randomly selected words being studied across content areas. This activity requires that students know specific attributes of the words in order to make potential connections. It also enhances students' creative thinking abilities as they consider subtle and imperceptible associations between two different terms.

Content Areas
All

Procedure
1. Select content vocabulary that students have recently learned.
2. Find other unrelated words, either selecting words randomly from a dictionary or using terms students are currently learning in another content area.
3. Write the words on cards and keep them in two separate piles.
4. Assign students to groups and have one group member randomly select a card from each pile.
5. Direct student groups to consider what they know about each term and what connections may be possible.
6. Have group members decide on one plausible connection to share with the class.

Example
An example of using terms across content areas follows.

HISTORY TERMS FOR A UNIT ON THE HOLOCAUST	SCIENCE TERMS FOR A UNIT ON AIR POLLUTION
racism	contaminants
propaganda	toxic
censorship	ambient air
disenfranchised	chronic
extermination	greenhouse gases
deportation	fossil fuels

Racism is vile and can hurt people. *Toxic* substances are vile and can hurt people.

Propaganda and *fossil fuels* both pollute. *Propaganda* pollutes information people receive and *fossil fuels* pollute the environment.

Censorship and *chronic*. *Censorship* and things that are *chronic* have the potential to influence outcomes over time.

Disenfranchised and *ambient air*. *Disenfranchised* people are marginalized (or external) in relation to a group of people considered mainstream. *Ambient air* is air that surrounds (or is external to) a given object.

Deportation and *greenhouse gases*. People who experience *deportation* are "expelled" from a certain place or country. *Greenhouse gases* are "expelled" from any kind of combustion engine, such as vehicles, lawnmowers, and other gas-driven machines.

Variations

- Forced associations can work well as a review and reinforcement activity.
- Students, especially English Language Learners, can use drawings to illustrate connections between terms.
- Students can create their own pairs of words for others to make associations.

S-11

POSSIBLE SENTENCES

Possible Sentences is a strategy that requires students to use the context of a selection to determine the appropriate meaning of key vocabulary words (Moore & Moore, 1986; Stahl & Kapinus, 1991). Students have to use the words in sentences that predict the content of the selection, then read the selection focusing on the use of the words in context; after reading, they modify their original sentences to coordinate with the manner in which the words were used in the text. This strategy has the potential to improve learning in the following ways:

- Aids retention and understanding through prediction and prior knowledge.
- Provides students with multiple exposures to key vocabulary before, during, and after the reading.
- Helps focus students' attention on the most significant concepts and their use in the context of a selection.

Materials
Overhead projector

Content Areas
All, except mathematics

Procedures

1. Select key vocabulary from the selection to be read and display them visually for students, on the board or an overhead projector. The list should contain both familiar and unfamiliar terms.

2. Ask students to make a sentence they predict could appear in the selection to follow using any two words. The sentence must reflect the syntax and content of the actual text itself and should not be personalized. For example, discourage personal sentences such as "I saw a picture of magma and a volcano on the Internet." It may be necessary for the teacher to "think aloud" and model one or more sentences for illustration purposes. You could start with something like "One possible sentence is: Volcanic bombs and cinders are dangerous byproducts of volcanic eruptions."

3. When you feel that students understand the kinds of sentences (usually after one or two "think alouds"), you can display the student-constructed sentences visually (on the overhead or the board) as they are developed.

4. Have students number their papers from 1-10, representing the total number of possible sentences constructed.

5. Next, direct students to read the selection with these sentences as their guide.

6. As they encounter each word during reading, tell students to mark with a T if the sentence is true according to the selection, an F if it is false, or DK if they do not know from the reading.

7. After the reading, call on students to read each sentence, and ask the class to tell where in the selection they encountered the word, how to modify the sentence to coordinate with the text, and what they think it means. For example, possible sentence #8 below reads "Composite cones hold the magma." You might say "Who can find the pages and paragraphs that talk about *composite cones*?" After calling on one student whose hand is raised, tell the class "Everyone go to page 214, as Robin indicated, and follow along while she reads aloud." Now, how might we change sentence #8 to reflect what the selection tells us about composite cones?" The students then modify the original sentence to "Composite cones are mountains with steep sides" as shown in the example.

8. Finally, you can review the key terms and ask the students to tell what each word means now that they have experienced the terms in the context of the selection.

Examples

LESSON: SCIENCE

I. *Prereading stage:* Teacher selected "key concepts"

Magma	Volcanic ash	Composite cones
Lava	Volcanologists	Pacific Ring of Fire
Volcano	Volcanic bombs	Aleutian Arc
Crater	Cinders	Rock
Vent	Cinder cones	
Volcanic dust	Shield Volcano	

Student Generated "Possible Sentences"

___ 1. *Magma* is hot, liquid *rock.*
___ 2. *Lava* flows out of the *crater.*
___ 3. *Volcanic bombs* come out of the *vent.*
___ 4. *Volcanologists* study *volcanoes.*
___ 5. *Volcanic dust* makes up the *Pacific Ring of Fire.*
___ 6. The *shield volcano* is tall so that it keeps the *magma* from coming out.
___ 7. *Volcanic Ash* comes out of the *vent.*
___ 8. *Composite cones* hold the *magma.*
___ 9. *Cinder cones* are small parts of a volcano shaped like *cones.*
___ 10. The *Aleutian Arc* is part of the *Pacific Ring of Fire.*

II. *Reading Stage*
    Tell the students that they are to read the selection on volcanos silently, keeping in mind their "possible sentences." As they read they are to label the possible sentences as T, F, or DK (if they aren't sure if the sentence is true or false). The students do not need to copy the sentences down, because they might not be true.

III. *Post-Reading Stage:* Sentences modified by students after reading.

___1. The center of the earth is composed of hot, liquid rock called magma.
___2. Lava flows out of the crater and cools as it is exposed to the atmosphere.
___3. Debris larger than 5 millimeters is called volcanic bombs.
___4. Scientists who study volcanoes are called volcanologists.
___5. Alaska lies along an area called the Pacific Ring of Fire.
___6. A shield volcano covers a large area, is dome-shaped, and has gently sloping sides.
___7. Volcanic ash is larger debris than volcanic dust, reaching up to 5 millimeters in size.
___8. Composite cones are mountains with steep sides.
___9. Cinder cones are small mountains with steep sides.
___10. Most of Alaska's volcanoes are located along the 1,500 mile Aleutian Arc which extends westward to Kamchatka and forms the northern part of the Pacific Ring of Fire.

Variations

- While introduced as a whole class activity, with practice, the strategy can be used in small groups or pairs to scaffold the learning and help students become more independent learners.
- To reinforce vocabulary knowledge, have students keep word banks of the terms discussed.

S-12

SEMANTIC MAPS

One of the most adaptable and multifaceted tools for promoting content vocabulary learning is the Semantic Map. Semantic Maps, which are visual displays that represent spatial relationships among words, have a strong research base to support their effectiveness (Baumann, Kamenuii, & Ash, 2003). This instructional technique requires students to activate background knowledge about a concept, move beyond definitions by categorizing words, and actively participate in class discussions about the concept. Semantic Maps work well as whole class, small group, and even individual activities to help students make associations, interact with text ideas, and respond personally to concepts. Furthermore, this activity can be used either before reading to help students draw on what they know about a topic and after reading to extend and reinforce learning.

Materials
Paper

Content Areas
All

Procedure

1. Begin by modeling how to create a semantic map. Use a simple concept such as "name people in the school." Write student responses and then think aloud as you determine categories for the names listed, such as teachers, administrators, custodians, or students). Then develop a semantic map to represent the information.
2. To begin the lesson, visually display the name of a topic (e.g., real numbers in mathematics; Nazi racism in a history class).
3. Have students brainstorm what they know about the term, and record their responses on either the chalkboard or on a transparency with an overhead projector.
4. Direct students to form small cooperative groups to categorize the terms generated by the class. By clustering the words into categories, students build a network of ideas to show the interrelationships and connections among concepts.
5. Bring the students back together as a whole class to discuss their maps.

Examples: Real numbers (before and during reading)

Nazi Racism (after reading)

Semantic Map
(before reading)

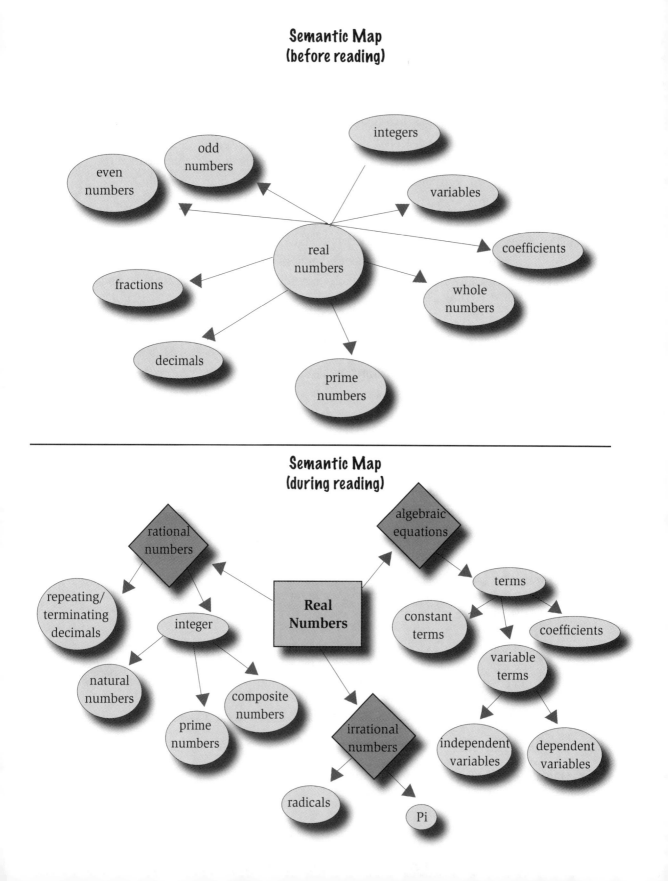

Semantic Map
(during reading)

SEMANTIC MAP
(after reading)

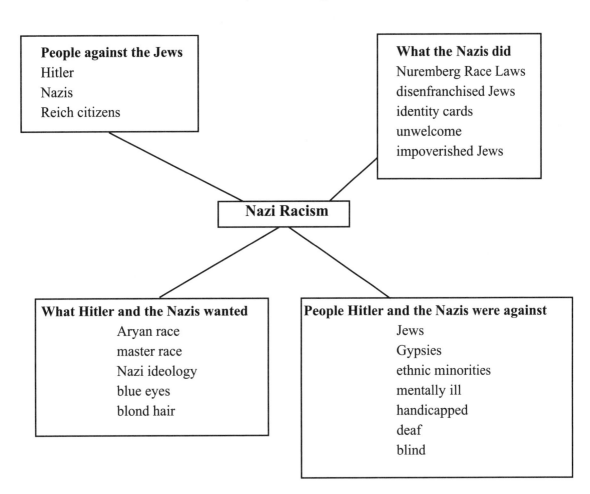

People against the Jews
Hitler
Nazis
Reich citizens

What the Nazis did
Nuremberg Race Laws
disenfranchised Jews
identity cards
unwelcome
impoverished Jews

Nazi Racism

What Hitler and the Nazis wanted
Aryan race
master race
Nazi ideology
blue eyes
blond hair

People Hitler and the Nazis were against
Jews
Gypsies
ethnic minorities
mentally ill
handicapped
deaf
blind

Variations

- As a prereading activity, students may begin the mapping and then add ideas to it as they read and learn about the topic.
- Semantic Maps can also be used after reading as a study technique to help students review and reinforce previously learned concepts.
- For students who have difficulty with reading, the teacher can suggest categories to get them started with their maps.
- During class discussions, you can ask directed questions to help students focus on the important aspects of the concept.
- Students can create their maps using a software program such as *Inspiration.*

S-13

CONCEPT CIRCLES

Concept Circles (Vacca & Vacca, 2005) help students relate words to one another by categories. The twist on Concept Circles is that the students are provided a visual, a circle divided into quadrants. Four related words are placed in the circle with one in each quadrant.

Materials
Blackline master of blank circles

Content Areas
All

Procedure
1. Choose four related words or phrases and place one in each quadrant.
2. Then ask the students to tell what category these words together might represent.

Example
Look at the following concept circle. Think about how these words are related and explain your answer under the circle.

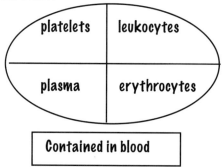

Variations
- Supply three words that are related in the circle and one that is not. Have students identify the three related words and discuss why they are related and why the fourth is not.
- Supply a category and then do not fill in any words; or supply some of the words for the quadrant and have students supply the rest of the words.
- Supply some related words in the circle and leave one or more sections to be filled in by students. Have students identify how these words in the completed circle are related.

CONCEPT CIRCLES

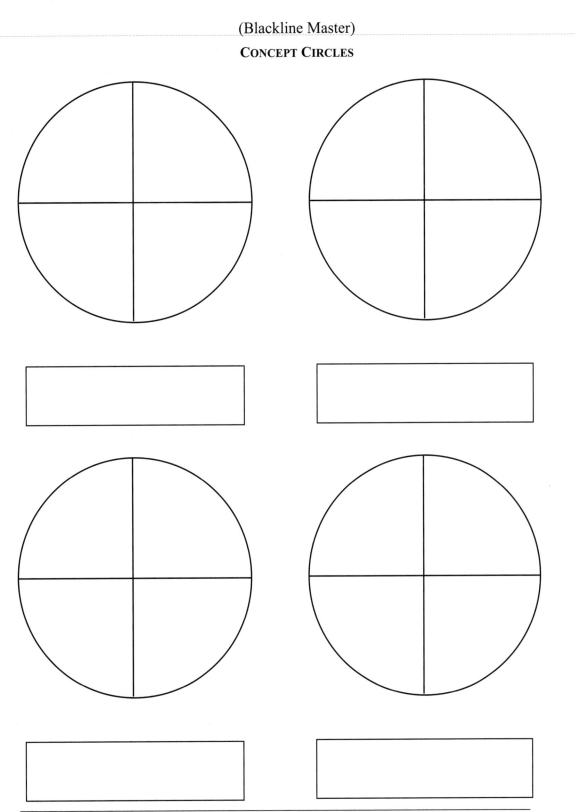

— 4 —

Clarifying Word Meanings

Many of the words found in specific content areas are *polysemous,* or multiple meaning, words that can be confusing to students. They may understand the typical meaning for "driver" but may be confused when they hear it used in reference to computers. Students can also get confused with many procedural phrases that are found in content area texts. Phrases, such as "composed primarily of" and "be adjacent to" can disrupt comprehension of text passages and cause much frustration for students, especially English Language Learners. Still other students may be uncertain about function words and phrases that signal special relationships, such as cause and effect, time order, and problem-solutions. The seven strategies identified below and described in this chapter are instructional tools that particularly address ways in which you can clarify word meanings for students through the use of contextual approaches and explicit instruction of multiple meaning and function words.

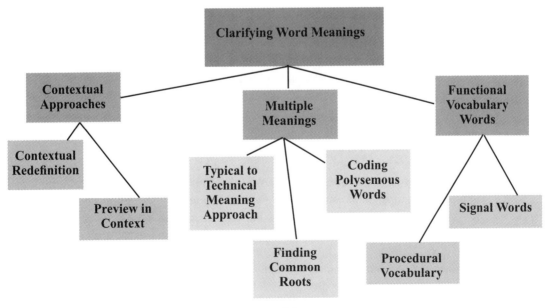

S-14

CONTEXTUAL REDEFINITION

The Contextual Redefinition strategy, described by Tierney and Readence (2000), is a teacher-directed, pre-reading activity for helping students use both context and their prior knowledge to figure out word meanings. This strategy helps students understand the following: (1) wild guessing at word meanings is not a productive strategy for unlocking the meanings of unfamiliar words; (2) context clues can provide important information about a word's meaning but should not be the only source of information; and (3) proficient readers use all accessible clues (i.e., word level, syntax, and semantics) to help them determine word meanings.

Materials
Contextual Redefinition Chart

Content Areas
All

Procedure

1. Identify several words students need to know to understand an assigned reading. These terms can be important for understanding the concepts addressed in the reading, or they can be words that your students may find difficult.

2. For each selected word, examine how the context in which it appears in the text may provide clues to the meaning of the word. If the context does not have enough information to help students gain some idea of the word's meaning, then write your own instructional context for the word.

3. Present the words to students in list form, pronouncing each word. Ask students to write the words in the first column of their chart. Pronounce the first word on the list again, and direct students to think about what the word might mean using their prior knowledge. Ask them to closely examine the word for possible meaning clues (e.g., prefixes, familiar roots); then ask for volunteers to guess the word's meaning and to support their guesses. Next, have students complete the second column of the chart.

4. Present the word in a strong context, using either the sentence from the text or the sentence you wrote. Read the sentence aloud and ask students to again think about the meaning of the word. Have students share their thoughts and support their ideas with sentence clues. Direct students to complete the third column.

5. Tell students to write a predicted meaning for the word in the fourth column. Then direct them to verify their predictions by checking in the textbook glossary or a dictionary to confirm their ideas. Students then write the actual word meaning in the final column.

Example

For a passage about earthquakes, the following words may be highlighted:
seismology, fault, tsunami

Instructional contexts for each word can be the following:

The history of *seismology* dates back to the 1750s when a major earthquake caused great damage to Lisbon, Portugal. This catastrophe prompted scientists of that time to learn more about earthquakes, including the effects, locations, and timing of these natural occurrences.

After the San Francisco earthquake of 1906, scientists learned that the forces that create earthquakes find weak areas in the earth's crust to relieve this gradual buildup of stress. These *fault* lines are sometimes located a great distance away from the source of the earthquake.

Coastal cities located in earthquake-prone areas are always in danger of the devastating effects of the ocean brought on by *tsunamis*.

Word	Word level clues	Context clues	Predicted word meaning	Actual word meaning
seismology	Clues: ology means "study of" Guess: study of something in science	Clues: earthquakes; learning more about earthquakes	study of earthquakes, including the effects, locations, and timing	study of earthquakes
fault	Clues: Guess: did something wrong	Clues: weak area	weak area in the earth's crust where an earthquake occurs	A fracture in the continuity of a rock formation caused by a shifting or dislodging of the earth's crust in which adjacent surfaces are displaced relative to one another and parallel to the plane of fracture.
tsunami	Clues: has "sun" in it Guess: sun has something to do with earthquakes	Clues: coastal cities; ocean	city flooded because of the water from the ocean	A very large ocean wave caused by an underwater earthquake or volcanic eruption.

Variations

- The Contextual Redefinition strategy can be conducted as class discussion without the use of the chart. However, the chart is useful for helping students understand the ways in which they can derive word meanings independently.
- Students can complete the chart in pairs or small groups before participating in a class discussion about the words.
- Students can select the words for this activity.

(Blackline Master)

CONTEXTUAL REDEFINITION CHART

Word	Word level clues	Context clues	Predicted word meaning	Actual word meaning
	Clues: Guess:	Clues:		
	Clues: Guess:	Clues:		
	Clues: Guess:	Clues:		
	Clues: Guess:	Clues:		

S-15

PREVIEW IN CONTEXT

Preview in Context is a technique for introducing new terms to students by using the actual contexts in which the students will encounter the words (Tierney, Readence, & Dishner, 2000). Using both prior knowledge and the passage context, the students and teacher investigate probable meanings for the targeted words and, through discussion, arrive at appropriate meanings.

Materials
List of targeted words; text passage

Content Areas
All

Procedure

1. Select 4-5 important vocabulary words from the text passage. Read the context to determine what clues are available that might help students understand the meaning of the targeted word.
2. Write the words on the board or on a transparency for students to view.
3. Pronounce the first word on the list. Ask if anyone knows something about the word.
4. Direct students to examine how the author uses the terms in the text passage. Read the section orally or have students read the section silently.
5. Begin a teacher-directed dialogue by asking a question, such as "What information does the sentence tell you about the word?" Subsequent questions to use in the discussion might be the following:
   a. Do you think this is enough information?
   b. What questions do you have about the word?
   c. Are there any word parts, such as prefixes or roots, that look familiar?
   d. What do these word parts tell us about the word?
   e. Can you think of a synonym for the word?
   f. Can you think of an antonym for the word?
   g. Given the information we have, what is a probable meaning for the word?
   h. Since the context does not provide us with enough information, let's use the dictionary.
   i. Compare the dictionary meaning with the way the author uses the word. Does it make sense?
6. Have students copy the definition in their notebook.

Example: Sample World History Lesson

TEXT PASSAGE

During the 1780s, France's government sank deeply into debt. *Extravagant* spending by the king and queen was part of the problem. Louis XVI, who became king in 1774, inherited part of the debt from his predecessors. He also borrowed heavily in order to help the American revolutionaries in their war against Great Britain—France's chief rival—thereby doubling the government's debt. In 1786, when bankers refused to lend the government any more money, Louis faced serious problems (Beck, Black, Krieger, Naylor, & Shabaka, 1999, p. 574).

T: Look at the word *extravagant*. From the way the author uses the word, what do you think it might mean?

S: It sounds like it has something to do with getting France into debt.

T: What makes you say that?

S: The first sentence says that the government was in debt; the second sentence says that the spending that the king and queen did was part of the problem. So maybe they spent too much money.

T: *Extravagant* has the prefix *extra* which means "to go beyond" or "to be outside of." Can you think of other words that begin with *extra?*

S. Extraordinary.

T: Good. What do you think *extraordinary* means?

S: Going what is beyond ordinary.

T: So how would you describe *extravagant* spending by the king and queen?

S: They spent more money than they had. They went beyond their means.

Variations

- Have pairs of students discuss possible word meanings before beginning the class discussion.
- Use semantic maps to help students visualize word meanings.
- Use student responses to assess their ability to use contextual clues.

S-16

TYPICAL TO TECHNICAL MEANING APPROACH

The Typical to Technical Meaning Approach, developed by Welker (1987) and promoted by Manzo, Manzo, and Thomas (2005) is designed to help students compare the common meanings of terms with their technical, content-specific meanings. This approach directs students to think carefully about the multiple meanings of a term. We have extended this approach to emphasize possible connections that can exist between the meanings.

Materials
Activity sheet

Content Areas
All

Procedure
1. Display targeted words on the chalkboard or overhead projector.
2. Ask students to share the first meaning that comes to mind when they see the term. Write these meanings on the chalkboard or overhead projector. Tell students that these meanings are called *typical* or *common meanings* for the terms.
3. Mention that common terms can hold different meanings when used in a specific content area. Discuss the technical meanings for the terms. Write these meanings on the chalkboard or use an overhead projector.
4. Ask students to think about how the meanings might be related.
5. Give each student a copy of the activity sheet. Working in pairs have students complete the meaning chart and sentence completions.
6. Discuss student answers.

Example: Computer terminology

COMPARING COMMON AND TECHNICAL MEANINGS

Word Meaning Chart: Write the typical meaning and technical meaning for each term below. Use the meanings below the chart to help you.

Term	Typical Meaning	Technical Meaning	Meaning Connections
queue			
firewall			
domain			
burn			
driver			

Which word is described?

- A person who operates a motorized vehicle   _____
- A fireproof wall that prevents a fire from spreading   _____
- To engrave a name on something   _____
- Land or territory that is ruled by someone   _____
- A line of people waiting for something   _____
- A file that helps a computer communicate and
  control a hardware device   _____
- To copy information to a CD   _____
- A network of computers that share a common address   _____
- A list of tasks that are waiting to be processed by a computer   _____
- Program used to protect a computer from unauthorized users   _____

Sentence Completions

Use a word from the chart to complete the sentences.

Movie goers had to form a _____ outside the ticket window in order to purchase tickets for the latest *Spiderman* movie.

Some hardware devices do not need a _____ for a computer to recognize and control them.

The absence of a _____ caused the building to burn to the ground.

My brother asked me to _____ a CD containing the latest photographs of our pet cat.

The king ruled over his _____ for twenty years before allowing any newcomers to settle on his land.

My printer had a _____ of documents waiting to be printed.

The young man's new Web site had a _____ of expert.com.

My computer is equipped with a _____ and is therefore protected from damage done by unauthorized users.

The images of war that were shown on TV are _____ in my memory.

The _____ of the car avoided hitting a deer by quickly moving into the left lane of traffic.

Variations
- Have students illustrate the common and technical word meanings.
- Challenge students to use both meanings of the same word in one sentence.
- Direct students to create their own sentence completions.

S-17

CODING POLYSEMOUS WORDS

Many words that appear in specific content areas are polysemous words—words that represent different meanings depending upon the discipline. For example, the word *tick* can mean the sound coming from a clock, but in a science class *tick* may refer to a small insect. Word coding is one technique for helping students distinguish the multiple meanings of polysemous words and to internalize these meanings. Based upon Paivio's idea of dual coding (1990) and what Strong, Perini, Silver, and Tuculescu (2002) describe as "Intensifying Vocabulary," the procedure presented below directs students to process information about a polysemous term in a variety of ways to reinforce learning.

Materials
Coding chart; polysemous words

Content Areas
All

Procedure

1. Highlight any polysemous word found in a passage that students will be reading.
2. Discuss the common meaning of the word with students and then present the specific content area meaning.
3. Direct students to work with a partner to complete the coding chart. (See example.)
4. Have students share their work in a whole class setting.

Example: Music

WORD: SCALE

Common meaning: device for measuring weight
Content meaning: series of musical steps

Code	Task
Visual code	Draw a musical scale.
Kinesthetic code	Play a musical scale on an instrument.
Social code	Play a musical scale with a partner.
Linguistic code	Write your own description of a musical scale.

Variations
- This technique will work with small groups as well as with partners.
- Students can use this type of coding to help them remember other difficult vocabulary terms that are not necessarily polysemous words.

(Blackline Master)

CODING POLYSEMOUS WORDS

WORD: _____

Common meaning: Content meaning:	
Code	**Task**
Visual code	
Kinesthetic code	
Social code	
Linguistic code	

Instructional Strategies for Teaching Content Vocabulary, Grades 4-12, by Janis M. Harmon, Karen D. Wood, and Wanda B. Hedrick. Published by National Middle School Association and International Reading Association. Copyright 2006 by National Middle School Association.

S-18

FINDING COMMON ROOTS

Students encounter many words in specific content areas that have multiple meanings. Some of these polysemous words can actually be homographs—words that have the same spellings but different meanings and different origins. This technique, Finding Common Roots, heightens students' interest about words as they investigate and compare the origins of multiple meaning words.

Materials
Finding Common Roots map

Content Areas
All

Procedure

1. Highlight any polysemous word that appears in the passage that students will read.
2. Discuss the common meaning of the word and the content-specific meaning of the word.
3. Point out that the word is called a "polysemous" word because it has different meanings and that it might be a homograph if the meanings have different origins. If the word is a homograph, then there will be separate entries in the dictionary for the meaning.
4. Direct students to work in pairs to discover if the targeted word is a homograph and to complete the Finding Common Roots map.
5. Have students discuss their findings as a whole class.

Example: Finding Common Roots

WORD: COMPOUND

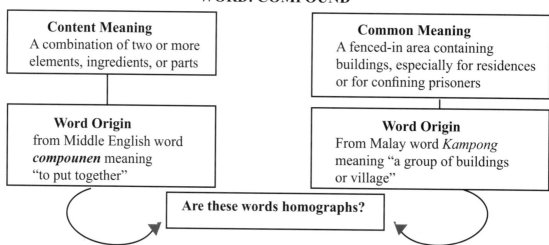

Content Meaning A combination of two or more elements, ingredients, or parts	**Common Meaning** A fenced-in area containing buildings, especially for residences or for confining prisoners
Word Origin from Middle English word ***compounen*** meaning "to put together"	**Word Origin** From Malay word *Kampong* meaning "a group of buildings or village"

Are these words homographs?

Variations
- Have students find other homographs by searching on the Internet.
- Display homographs on a word wall in the classroom.

(Blackline Master)

FINDING COMMON ROOTS

WORD: _____

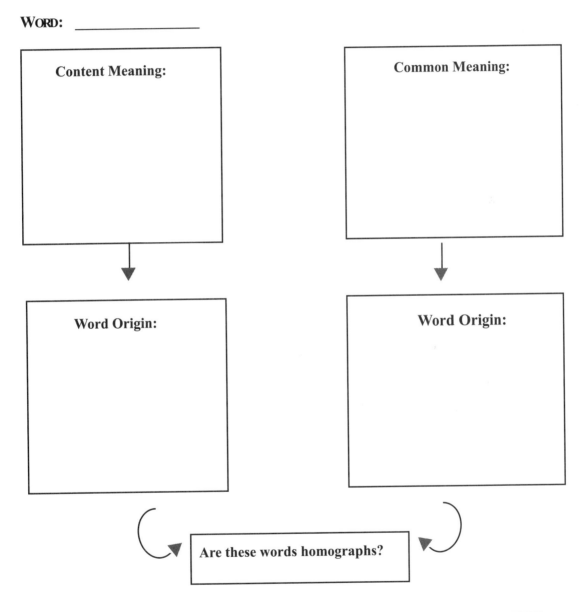

| Content Meaning: | Common Meaning: |

| Word Origin: | Word Origin: |

Are these words homographs?

Instructional Strategies for Teaching Content Vocabulary, Grades 4-12, by Janis M. Harmon, Karen D. Wood, and Wanda B. Hedrick. Published by National Middle School Association and International Reading Association. Copyright 2006 by National Middle School Association.

S-19

PROCEDURAL VOCABULARY

The technical vocabulary terms of a specific content vocabulary, such as the sciences, are not the only words that may present difficulties for struggling readers, especially students who are learning English as a second language. There are many function words and phrases in content texts that we may assume every student understands. These function words indicate special relationships among concepts and ideas, such as *corresponds to, can be distinguished from, consists of,* and *are the result of.* Because these phrases signal the manner in which content ideas are related, students need to know what they mean in order to develop the appropriate and correct understandings about the concept.

Marco and Luzon (1999) categorize these phrases into nine distinct areas: (1) phrases that identify the similarities between concepts; (2) phrases that indicate differences between concepts; (3) inclusion phrases that show how one concept may be part of another; (4) exclusion phrases that show how one concept is not part of something else; (5) phrases that signal the process that links two concepts; (6) phrases that indicate the function or use of concepts; (7) phrases about spatial relations that indicate the location of a concept in relation to another; (8) phrases signaling physical characteristics in terms of size, dimension, and appearance; and (9) phrases that indicate quantity. Examples of each category are provided below.

Content Areas
Physical Science
Biology
Chemistry
Health

Procedure

1. Examine the chapter or text section that students will be reading in an upcoming lesson. In addition to examining the technical vocabulary load of the passage, also attend to procedural vocabulary phrases. In our example of the passage "Hair and Nails," below, we noted six procedural vocabulary phrases that may be stumbling blocks for struggling readers.

   is produced by   *that extends beyond*
   that extend into   *consists mostly of*
   surrounding the   *are composed primarily of*

2. Write the phrases on a transparency or chalkboard. Below each phrase write the phrase in a sentence about a topic that the students will understand. Examples:

is produced by
Milk *is produced by* cows.

that extend into
Plants have roots *that extend into* the soil.

surrounding the
The fans *surrounding the* famous pop singer all wanted an autograph.

that extends beyond
The part of a hamburger *that extends beyond* the bun is usually eaten first.

consists mostly of
My favorite salad *consists mostly of* spinach, tomatoes, and black olives.

are composed primarily of
I like cookies that *are composed primarily of* white chocolate chips, pecans, and less dough.

3. Discuss the purpose of the phrase and why an author might use it in the passage.
is produced by—illustrate process

that extend into—show spatial relationship

surrounding the—show spatial relationship

that extends beyond—show spatial relationship

consists mostly of—defines the whole in terms of the parts

are composed primarily of—defines the whole in terms of the parts

4. Direct students to the sentence in the text that contains the phrase. Discuss the meaning that the author is trying to convey.

5. Remind students to pay attention to the phrases as they read.

Example Passage

HAIR AND NAILS*

Hair *is produced by* cells at the base of the hair follicles, deep pockets *that extend into* the dermis. Blood vessels *surrounding the* hair follicles nourish the hair root. The shaft of hair *that extends beyond* the skin *consists mostly of* keratin and requires no nourishment. Oil secreted by glands in the skin prevents the shaft from drying out and breaking off. Individual hairs usually grow for several years and then fall out. However, hair on the scalp can grow continuously for many years.

Nails, which protect the ends of the fingers and toes, form from cells at the end of a deep fold of epidermis. As new cells form at the base of the nail, the nail grows longer. Like hair, nails *are composed primarily of* keratin. (p. 650)

---

*Taken from *Modern Biology*. (1991). Austin, TX: Holt, Rinehart and Winston, Inc.

Variations

- Pair familiar phrases with the phrases used in the text. For example, for the phrase *consists of* use the phrase *is made up of* as a synonym.
- Have students substitute different phrases in the passage.
- Use illustrations to demonstrate the relationships signified by the phrases.

PROCEDURAL VOCABULARY CHART (adapted from Marco & Luzon, 1999)

Similarities

be similar to	be counterpart of	be equivalent to	be considered
be like	corresponding	be equal to	be interpreted as
look like	match	be an equivalent of	be regarded as
resemble	be proportional to	be indistinguishable	be thought of as
approximate	a kind of	from	share
approach	correspond to	be synonymous with	be akin to
be identical with/to	be analogous to	be the same as	be comparable to

Difference

be different from	be distinguished from
as opposed to	be opposite
be dissimilar	be unlike
be distinct from	differ from

Inclusion

be a member of	be a case of	be exemplified by	be an example of
be a kind of	be a class of	as illustrated by	be a prototype of
be a type of	be a form of	be represented by	be representative of
belong to	be a variant of	be a component of	range from…to…
fall into	be composed of	be an element of	vary from…to…
be divided/subdivided	be comprised of	be part of	be provided with
into	be filled with	be made from	comprise
be equipped with	be formed by	be made up of	consist of
contain	be a piece of	be a portion of	appear in
encompass	be a fragment of	be characteristic of	

Exclusion

be absent from
be excluded from
to the exclusion of
be devoid of
be free of
lack
missing

Process relationships

arise from	come from	originate from	give way to
be a derivative of	derive from	give rise to	yield
be a product of	develop from	be the result of	are the result of
be due to	be produced by/from	result from	be converted to
become		branch into	evolve into
transform into			

Function

act as	provide
act to	serve as
behave like	be useful for
function as	be used for
have a role in	be chosen as
play the role of	employ as
play a part in	is used to

Spatial relationships

be adjacent to	be distributed	be located	extend
be arranged	be embedded in	be placed	face
be contained in	be equidistant	be positioned at	opposite
be coated with	be parallel to	be separated	reside
be covered with	be inserted into	be surrounded by	surround

Physical characteristics

be...in length
in the form of
shape like
in shades of
measuring more than
(noun)-shaped

Quantity

a variety of
amounts of
number of
(cardinal number) parts of
a class of
a family of
a series of
a set of

Source: Marco, M., & Luzon, M. (1999). Procedural vocabulary: Lexical signaling of conceptual relations in discourse. *Applied Linguistics, 20*(1), 1-21. Used by permission of Oxford University Press.

S-20

SIGNAL WORDS

Teaching students about the text structures that authors use to write texts can enhance comprehension. For specific text structures, including cause and effect, comparison-contrast, description, sequence, and problem-solution, authors use certain words and phrases, called signal words, that help the reader understand how the information is organized. Familiarity with signal words enables readers to recognize text structures that appear in different content area textbooks.

Materials
Blank chart containing types of text structures

Content Areas
All

Procedure
1. Discuss text structures with students and show them examples of each type of text structure. Be sure to emphasize that authors may use a variety of text structures in their writing.
2. Select a passage that is representative of one text structure. Read the passage orally to students and highlight any signal words as you read.
3. Tell students that these highlighted words are signal words because they provide clues to the type of text structure in the passage.
4. Show examples of other text structures using excerpts from student textbooks.
5. Have students complete the chart by adding signal words under the appropriate text structure heading.

Example: Several text structures:

TEXT PASSAGE: THE ALLIES STRIKE BACK

After a string of victories, the Japanese seemed unbeatable. *Nonetheless*, the Allies—mainly Americans and Australians—were anxious to strike back in the Pacific. In April 1942 the United States wanted revenge for Pearl Harbor. *So* the United States sent 16 B-25 bombers under the command of Lieutenant Colonel James H. Doolittle to bomb Tokyo and other major Japanese cities. The bombs did little damage. The attack, *however*, made an important psychological point: the Japanese could be attacked. (Beck, Black, Krieger, Naylor, & Shabaka, 1999, p. 829)

> T: Look at the first sentence in this passage. The word *after* signals that one thing happened before another. What happened first?
> S: The Japanese had many victories.

T: So this sentence represents a sequence of events text structure. Follow along as I read the next sentence. Now what is the author telling us?

S: That even though the Japanese might be hard to beat, we still wanted to strike back.

T: That's correct. So we actually have two opposite ideas here—the Japanese seemed to be too strong to beat, and the United States wanted to fight back. The word *nonetheless* is a signal word that tells us that we will be reading about two contrasting ideas. Another word that does the same thing—tells us about two contrasting ideas— is the word *however* in the last sentence. What are the opposing ideas?

S: The Tokyo bombings did not do much damage, but we found out that we could attack Japan, and that was encouraging.

SIGNAL WORDS CHART

Sequence (time order)	Description and Main Idea and Supporting Details	Cause and Effect and Problem-Solution	Comparison and Contrast
first second third finally next as now on (specific date) when after before previously currently in the future later	for example for instance most importantly in addition furthermore	so so that because since if…then therefore due to as a result nevertheless thus in spite of	but on the other hand however nonetheless not only…but also yet while either…or neither…nor although while in contrast to compared to unless although similar to more than less than

Variations

- Have students use the signal words as they write passages that represent different text structures.
- Create word games that require students to match signal words and phrases with appropriate text structures.
- Post the signal words on a word wall for easy reference.

(Blackline Master)

SIGNAL WORDS CHART

Sequence (time order)	Description and Main Idea and Supporting Details	Cause and Effect and Problem-Solution	Comparison and Contrast

Instructional Strategies for Teaching Content Vocabulary, Grades 4-12, by Janis M. Harmon, Karen D. Wood, and Wanda B. Hedrick. Published by National Middle School Association and International Reading Association. Copyright 2006 by National Middle School Association.

Identifying and Remembering Terms

In any content area, students will learn a multitude of new terms representing both familiar and unfamiliar concepts and even difficult, complex ideas. For some students, being able to hold on to these newly learned ideas and terms requires more effort and time. These students need "hooks" to help them as they apply the knowledge they have learned to more sophisticated concepts. This chapter emphasizes the use of nine visualization tactics and mnemonic devices identified in the graphic below to provide students with independent strategies for helping them identify and remember terms.

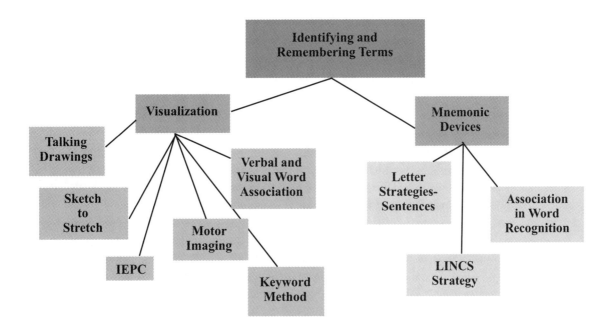

S-21

TALKING DRAWINGS

Talking Drawings is a strategy in which students draw pictures of their mental images of a topic, character, or event before reading a selection (Wood, 2001). Students then talk about and analyze their drawings with a partner. After reading the selection, the students construct another drawing that depicts their newly learned knowledge. The purpose of Talking Drawings is to

- Promote the use of mental imagery.
- Help students make connections with a given topic.
- Improve understanding and recall of a given topic.

Materials
Selected passage, chapters, or a combination
of multiple sources

Content Areas
All

Procedure

1. Have students close their eyes and imagine the topic, event, or character to be studied. Then tell them to open their eyes and draw what they saw in their minds.
2. Have the students share their drawings with at least two other students. Ask them to talk about and analyze why they depicted the topic as they did.
3. Have the students share their thinking and drawing with the whole class, explaining personal experiences and sources of information that helped them create their drawings.
4. Create a concept map or cluster of information on the board or on an overhead transparency using contributions from the class discussion.
   1. *Reading stage:* Have the students read the selected passage or chapter with their drawings in mind.
   2. *Post-reading stage:* In small groups or as a whole class discuss the selection and have students develop new drawings or change existing drawings to correspond with information gleaned from the passage and the discussion.
   3. Finally, have students share and compare their before and after drawings with partners or group members, discussing the reasons for the changes they made to their drawings. Encourage them to return to the selection and read aloud specific passages that support the changes they made.

Example: Biology: The Circulation System

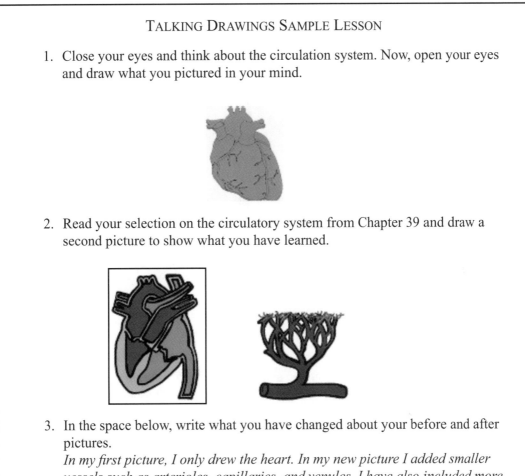

TALKING DRAWINGS SAMPLE LESSON

1. Close your eyes and think about the circulation system. Now, open your eyes and draw what you pictured in your mind.

2. Read your selection on the circulatory system from Chapter 39 and draw a second picture to show what you have learned.

3. In the space below, write what you have changed about your before and after pictures.

   In my first picture, I only drew the heart. In my new picture I added smaller vessels such as arterioles, capillaries, and venules. I have also included more details in the heart such as the Pulmonary vein and artery and the different chambers in my second drawing.

Variations

- Students may be asked to *write* what changes they made from one drawing to the next.
- The new learning can be extended by having the students further research related topics.
- The "after" reading drawings may be completed in partners or groups.

S-22

SKETCH TO STRETCH

Sketch to Stretch (Tierney & Readence, 2000) is a strategy intended to help students use drawings or sketches as a method of exploring, expressing, and sharing interpretations of selections. This strategy

- Allows for the generation of new meanings and insights that may not be captured in verbal responses.
- Helps students understand that different readers have different responses and interpretations of a text.
- Provides opportunities for students to share and react to one another's work.

Materials
Selected text passage, chapters, or a combination of multiple sources

Content Areas
All

Procedure

1. Have students read the selected text.
2. Ask students to think about the selection and draw a sketch of what the passage meant to them or what they were able to learn from the selection. Be sure to do the following:
   - Encourage students to experiment.
   - Remind them that there are many different ways to express meaning.
   - Help students focus on interpretation instead of artistic ability.
   - Provide them with ample time so they are not rushed.
   - Provide examples of sketches for students to see.
     1. Place students in groups of four or five.
     2. Have each student in the group share his or her sketch with group members. Note: Instruct the student who did the sketch not to verbalize his or her interpretation.
     3. Have the other students in the group say what they think the artist is trying to say in his or her picture.
     4. Once everyone in the group has a chance to suggest an interpretation, the artist can give his or her interpretation. Each member of the group needs to share in this manner.
     5. Have each group select one sketch to share with the entire class. Follow the same sharing process as above.

Example: World History: The Bubonic Plague

SAMPLE ONE: THE BUBONIC PLAGUE

SAMPLE TWO: THE BUBONIC PLAGUE

Variations:

- Students may add to or change their drawings after a second reading of the text.
- Students may develop sketches for other related texts.
- Students may use sketches in conjunction with drafting, presenting written texts, and written projects.
- The sketches may be used in a class book.
- Students may draw their sketches on overhead transparencies instead of paper to share with the class.

SAMPLE ESSAY

Just mention the name and you will send shivers down the spine of many people.

There is no doubt that this disease was deadly. Deadly and gruesome to watch.

The death rate was 90% for those exposed to the bacterium. It was transmitted by fleas from infected rats. The symptoms were clear: swollen lymph nodes (buboes, hence the name), high fever, and delirium. In the worst cases, the lungs became infected and the pneumonic form was spread from person to person by coughing, sneezing, or simply talking.

From the time of infection to death was less than one week.

There were three major epidemics—in the 6th, 14th, and 17th centuries.

The death toll was 137 million victims.

As a result, the plague is considered to be the worst epidemic of all time, but it wasn't (not that we are downplaying the severity of the plague).

At its worst, the Bubonic Plague killed two million victims a year.

$$\boxed{\textbf{S-23}}$$

IMAGINE, ELABORATE, PREDICT, AND CONFIRM (IEPC)

IEPC (Wood & Endres, 2005) is a strategy intended to help students increase their understanding and recall by using visual imagery to predict events in a selection. The strategy will

- Encourage students to use visual imagery.
- Encourage the use of prior knowledge.
- Help them improve prediction skills.
- Help them improve recall and understanding.

Materials
Selected text passage, chapters, or a combination of multiple sources

Content Areas
All

Procedure
1. Choose a selection with content appropriate for visual imagery.
2. Display the blank IEPC form on an overhead projector; tell students that they are going to use a strategy designed to encourage them to use their imaginations to create pictures in their mind to help them understand and remember what they read.
3. Use a transparency to point out and explain the four phases of IEPC using language that is appropriate to their ability levels.
4. *Prereading Stage:* Have students read or hear a selection. Begin with the *imagine* phase and ask the students to close their eyes and imagine everything they can about the selection to be read. This may be based on the cover of the book, a title, or a topic. Encourage students to imagine feelings, taste, smell, sight, and surroundings. You do the same.
   a. Model this strategy by talking aloud about your thinking.
   b. Ask students if they have anything to add. Write responses in the "I" column.
   c. Model how to use their visual images to add details, anecdotes, prior experiences, and sensory information. Write this information in the "E" column.
   d. Talk about at least one sample prediction based on prior visual images, and encourage students to do the same. Write responses in the "P" column.
5. *Reading Stage:* Have students read or listen to the selection with the above predictions in mind.
6. *Post-Reading Stage:* After reading, return to the transparency and modify the original predictions using a different color marker. Write down student responses and confirmations in the "C" column on the transparency.

Example: Economic, Legal, and Political Systems: Voting

IMAGINE, ELABORATE, PREDICT, AND CONFIRM (IEPC)
Sample student responses: Topic: "Voting"

I	E	P	C
IMAGINE: Close your eyes and imagine the given topic. What do you see, feel, hear, smell?	ELABORATE: Tell, describe, give details of what you "see" in your mind.	PREDICT: Use your images and ideas to make some predictions about the passage you will read.	Read to CONFIRM or change your predictions about the passage.
Presidents and other politicians *People in line waiting to vote.*	*I hear speeches and debates.* *I see posters outside the building with "Democrat" and "Republican" slogans.* *I see ads on T.V. for weeks before the election.* *I feel anxious.*	*I predict that this passage will be about elections and how voting works.* *Political parties.*	*The chapter was about registering to vote, the electoral college and how voting works, and why people should vote.* *New words:* *Electorate – the people who are eligible to vote* *Apathy – lack of interest*

Variations

- Ask students to provide page numbers or specific quotes from the text that support their confirmations.
- Ask students to actually draw their images on paper before and after reading.
- Have students work in pairs or groups during the post-reading stage to make confirmations.

(Blackline Master)

IMAGINE, ELABORATE, PREDICT, AND CONFIRM (IEPC)

I	E	P	C

S-24

MOTOR IMAGING

Motor Imaging is a strategy that uses physical-sensory skills to help teach new vocabulary words (Manzo & Manzo, 2001). The strategy will
- Help students retain and recall vocabulary words.
- Include multiple learning styles.

Materials
Selected text passage, chapters, or list of vocabulary words

Content Areas
All

Procedure
1. Take a difficult word from the text and write it on the board or overhead projector. Pronounce the word and give its meaning.
2. Ask students to imagine a simple pantomime or gesture for the word meaning. Ask how they could "show" someone what the word means.
3. Give students an agreed upon signal and have them do their pantomimes simultaneously.
4. Note the most common gesture used. Demonstrate to the class selected pantomime.
5. Have students repeat the word and pantomime with you.
6. Repeat each new word and direct the class to do the pantomime and simultaneously recite a brief meaning or synonym.

Example: Geometry: Polygons

MOTOR IMAGING – SAMPLE GEOMETRY LESSON

New Word	Language Meaning	Motor Meaning
polygon	*A polygon is formed by 3 or more coplanar sides. Polygon sides that have common endpoints are noncollinear, and each side intersects exactly 2 other sides, but only at their endpoints.*	*Elbows out—hands in—middle fingers of hands touching in front of body.*
convex	*A polygon is convex if any line containing a side of the polygon does not contain a point in the interior of the polygon.*	*Straight hands, middle fingers touching and pointing away from the body like an arrow.*
concave	*A polygon is concave if a line containing a side of the polygon contains a point in the interior of the polygon.*	*Opposite of convex. Straight hands, middle fingers touching and pointing in towards the body like an arrow.*
vertex	*A vertex of a polygon is where three or more edges intersect at a point.*	*Hold up index finger of left hand and index and middle finger of right hand. Bring all three fingers together.*
edges	*An edge of a polygon is where pairs of faces intersect at line segments.*	*Hold left hand vertically, fingers pointing away from body. Hold right hand horizontally, fingers pointing away from body. Bring edges of hands together to form what resembles a shelf.*

Variations
- Have each student create his or her own gesture to accompany a given word.
- Allow students to work in pairs or groups to create appropriate pantomimes for words.

(Blackline Master)

MOTOR IMAGING

New Word	Language Meaning	Motor Meaning

S-25

KEYWORD METHOD

The Keyword Method (Foil & Alber, 2002; Mastropieri & Scruggs, 1998) is a mnemonic strategy for elaborating upon an unfamiliar word or concept by making it more meaningful and concrete. The strategy will
- Help students with recall of vocabulary and concepts.
- Help students with the retention of vocabulary and concepts.

Materials
Selected text passage, chapter,
or list of vocabulary words and concepts

Content Areas
All

Procedure
1. Introduce the strategy to students. Explain that the strategy is intended to help them learn and remember new and unfamiliar terms.
2. *Recording Step:* Tell the student to change the unfamiliar word to a similar sounding familiar word that is easily pictured.
3. Advise students to practice saying the vocabulary and keyword together to establish an association.
4. *Relating Stage:* Tell students to form a visual image or draw a picture in which the keyword and the meaning of the vocabulary word are interacting.
5. *Retrieving Stage:* When students are asked to provide the definition of the vocabulary word, remind them to think of the picture involving the vocabulary word and the keyword in order to retrieve the definition from the picture.

Example: Math: Geometry

KEYWORD METHOD: GEOMETRY SAMPLE LESSON

Vocabulary

Word	Definition	Keyword	Explanation	Image
fractals	shapes that are irregular or broken	*fractured bone*	*Fractals are broken shapes —fractured bones are broken bones.*	*Broken bones of all different shapes.*
coplanar	points on the same plane	*co-pilot*	*Coplanar refers to points on the same plane—co-pilots fly the same plane.*	*Two pilots flying a plane with a geometric plane below it.*
acute angle	angle whose degree measure is less than 90	*a cute angel*	*Acute angles are small—and cute angels are small too.*	*A little angel with a skirt drawn like an angle.*
hemisphere	each great circle separates a plane into two congruent parts called hemispheres	*half-a-sphere*	*Hemi-sphere refers to half a sphere.*	*A circle cut into two pieces.*
obtuse angle	angle whose degree measure is greater than 90	*moose angle*	*Obtuse angles are big—A large moose is big too.*	*A moose with an angle drawn between his antlers*

Variations
- Students may work in pairs or groups to collaborate on keywords and images.
- Students may share their keywords with a group or whole class.

(Blackline Master)

KEYWORD METHOD

Word	Definition	Keyword	Explanation	Image

S-26

VERBAL AND VISUAL WORD ASSOCIATION

Verbal and Visual Word Association is a strategy that helps students learn and retain vocabulary words independently (Readence, Bean, & Baldwin, 2000). This strategy will
- Encourage students to make personal connections to the word.
- Provide a way to easily organize and visualize thoughts about a word.

Materials
Selected text passage, chapters, or a list of vocabulary words

Content Areas
All

Procedure
1. Have students draw a simple box with four boxes in it.
2. Have students write the new vocabulary word in the upper left box.
3. Have them write the word's definition in the bottom left box.
4. Now have them think of a personal association with the given word and write it in the upper right box.
5. Lastly, ask students to think of an experience or association that is NOT associated with the given vocabulary word.

Example: Spanish vocabulary

VERBAL AND VISUAL WORD ASSOCIATION SAMPLE: SPANISH VOCABULARY

Verbal

Lo estan pasando muy bein.	*Birthday party, mall, hanging out with friends*
They are having a good time.	*Doing chores, going to the dentist*

Variations

To include the *visual* portion of the strategy:

1. Write the word in the upper left box.
2. Write the definition in the lower left box.
3. Draw a picture or symbol of the word in the upper right box.
4. Write a verbal personal association in the lower right box.

Visual

ambicoso	
hardworking	*my father*

S-27

LETTER STRATEGIES—SENTENCES

Mnemonic strategies are systematic procedures intended to improve memory and recall. More specifically, Letter Strategies—Sentences is a method for remembering lists of terms or ideas in a specific order (Mastropieri & Scruggs, 1998). This strategy will
- Encourage student creativity.
- Improve recall and retention of words and terms.

Materials
Selected text passage, chapters, or a list of vocabulary words

Content Areas
All

Procedure
1. Identify the list of words or objects students need to know in a specific order. Make sure all students are familiar with each word.
2. Have students list the first (lead) letter of each word down the margin of their paper.
3. Tell students to write a new word beginning with the same letter next to each lead letter on the page. The new words should form a silly but easy-to-remember sentence.
4. Tell students to share their sentences with a partner and practice saying their sentences for retention.

Example: Economic, Legal, and Political Systems: The Bill of Rights

LETTER STRATEGIES – SENTENCES SAMPLE LESSON

THE BILL OF RIGHTS

Amendment	Key Word	New Word for Sentence
1	**Freedoms**	*Fresh*
2	Right to bear **arms**	*Amelia*
3	No soldiers **quartered** in homes	*quietly*
4	No unreasonable **search** and seizure	*sneaks*
5	Protects the rights of those **accused** of crimes	*around*
6	Rights for those accused of crimes – right to a **jury**	*joking and*
7	Right to a jury in **civil** cases	*carrying*
8	Forbids cruel and unusual **punishments**	*pretty*
9	**Unwritten** rights cannot be taken away	*underwear and*
10	Gives power to the **states**	*socks.*

New Sentence. *Fresh Amelia quietly sneaks around joking and carrying pretty underwear and socks.*

Variations

- Students may work in groups or pairs to create their sentences.
- Students may illustrate their new sentences.

(Blackline Master)

LETTER STRATEGIES

Term	Key Word	New Word for Sentence

Instructional Strategies for Teaching Content Vocabulary, Grades 4-12, by Janis M. Harmon, Karen D. Wood, and Wanda B. Hedrick. Published by National Middle School Association and International Reading Association. Copyright 2006 by National Middle School Association.

S-28

LINK, IMAGINE, NOTE, CONSTRUCT, SELF-TEST (LINCS)

The LINCS strategy (Ellis, 1992; Foil & Alber, 2002) is a way for students to independently generate keywords for target vocabulary. This strategy provides a systematic way for students to learn and understand new vocabulary words.

Materials
Selected text passage, chapters, or list of key vocabulary words

Content Areas
All

Procedure

1. *List* the parts. Ask students to write the word on an index card and list the most important parts of the definition on the back.
2. *Imagine.* Tell them to imagine a picture that depicts the word and describe it in their head or to a partner.
3. *Note* a reminding word. Have students think of a familiar word that sounds like the vocabulary word or has similar meaning and write it on the bottom half of the front of their index card.
4. *Construct* a LINCing story. Students make up a short story or sentence about the meaning of the word that includes the reminding word.
5. *Self-test.* Students test their memory using their index cards.

Example: Spanish I vocabulary

LINCS SAMPLE LESSON: SPANISH VOCABULARY

Word	L	I	N	C	S Did you get it right?
el/la amigo(a)	friend	*a high school age girl*	*Amelia – my best friend*	*Amelia is my amiga.*	+
el arbol	tree	*the big tree in my backyard*	*Arbor Day*	*I looked at el arbol at the Arbor Day Festival.*	+
a boca	mouth	*a big smile*	*Boca Burgers*	*You eat Boca Burgers with la boca.*	—
la carta	letter	*a stamped, addressed envelope*	*card*	*My birthday card is la carta I got in the mail!*	+
la madre	mother	*my mom*	*mad*	*La madre is always mad!*	+

Variations

- Students may create cards in groups or with partners.
- Students may make mini-posters with illustrations for each new word.
- Students may use charts instead of index cards.

LINCS

Word	L	I	N	C	S

S-29

ASSOCIATION IN WORD RECOGNITION

Developed by Punch and Robinson (1992), the Association in Word Recognition approach is designed to help students understand and remember content vocabulary. The technique is based upon the learning principle that meaningful learning occurs when students are able to make associations between their prior knowledge and experiences and new information. Because the level of abstractness and complexity of new terms in content areas can constrain learning, students may need extra support to retain word meanings. The Association in Word Recognition approach allows students to learn new words through meaningful connections embedded in the words. We realize that not all words will work, but for those words that do work, this activity provides an interesting mnemonic device to use.

Materials
List of vocabulary terms

Content Areas
All

Procedures
1. Select important terms that students need to know to understand a text passage.
2. Carefully study the spellings of the words to see if there are smaller words within the terms that can be used to make an association with the word's meaning.
3. Develop an explanation that shows the connection between the smaller word and the actual vocabulary term.

Examples: Social Studies Terms (from Punch & Robinson, 1992, © National Council for the Social Studies. Reprinted by permission)

SOCIAL STUDIES TERMS

American
   Note the *I can* at the end. Expand this to how the American psyche is success oriented. In a free society, we are free to explore our interests and potentials—our "I can." I can explore; I can enjoy freedom; I can succeed; I am an American.

Amendment
   To *mend.* To fix. To change. Ask students to think of this connection in the center of amendment. Students connect it to a change that adds or takes out part, as in the Bill of Rights and other amendments to the U.S. Constitution. A mend. A change. To improve.

Segregate

Note the word *gate* which means to separate or keep apart. This word connection provides a classic example for discussion of and learning about this word and its meaning. The teacher could construct a cardboard gate in the classroom for demonstration purposes, selecting students to play groups of people who are excluded, or kept apart, from others.

Monopoly

The vowel *o* has exclusive control in the word monopoly; it contains no other vowels (discounting the y at the end of the word). Use this device to reflect on the fact that a monopoly is a business with no competition; exclusive control of a product or service is held by one company. (pp. 402-403)

MATHEMATICS TERMS

Perimeter

The word perimeter contains the small word *rim*. Ask students to think about how the rim of a glass is the outside edge. Have them make the connection to perimeter which is the sum of the sides of a polygon.

Horizontal

A horizontal line looks like the horizon in the sky; goes in the same direction as the crossed line in H and the crossed line in T.

Measurement

Measurement has the word *sure* in it. Think about how measurements are sure things. You are sure of your numbers if you have measured correctly.

Variations

- Have students look for small words within terms and then create their own explanations.
- Direct students to create visual representations to illustrate the connection between the actual term and the smaller word.

— 6 —

Examining Word Parts

A high percentage of words found in the content areas contain meaningful roots and affixes that represent the same meaning across different contexts. By emphasizing these meaningful word parts, teachers help students develop a powerful, independent word learning strategy that is transferable to many word learning opportunities. For example, students who recognize that the Greek root "bios" refers to life will be better prepared to understand words such as *biology* (study of life), *biography* (written story of a person's life), *bionic* (having to do with life), and *antibiotic* (against living things that attack the body). This chapter offers six practical activities that work well in all content areas.

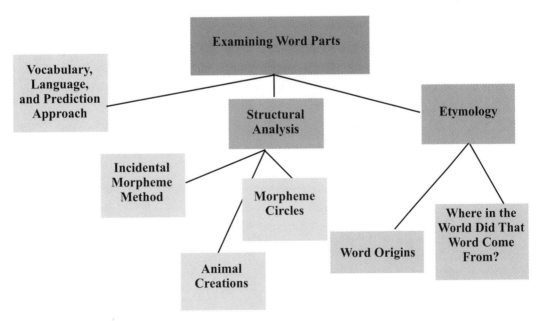

$$\boxed{S\text{-}30}$$

VOCABULARY, LANGUAGE, AND PREDICTION APPROACH

This strategy (Wood & Robinson, 1983; Wood, Harmon, & Hedrick, 2004) engages students in various aspects of word study (structural analysis, morphology) by providing practice, familiarity, and multiple exposures to significant vocabulary in a game-like manner. The Vocabulary, Language, and Prediction (VLP) Approach has as its basis the need to pre-teach and reinforce vocabulary, the role of oral language and word study in comprehension, and the importance of prediction in promoting understanding.

Materials
Text passages

Content Areas
All

Procedure

1. For the preparation stage, analyze the selection and determine which words represent the major content, events, and concepts and warrant further explanation.
2. Next, decide on questions to ask about these words that relate to various word study elements such as structural analysis—questions about prefixes, suffixes, and roots; antonyms; synonyms; categorization; syllables; parts of speech, such as adverbs, nouns, and adjectives.
3. Then display the words visually for the students, and tell them that they will be asking questions about the meaning and various features of the words as a means of familiarizing themselves with the terms before reading. With a small group of students, the words can be put on cards and placed on a table for them to select. With an entire class, the students can write the words on separate pieces of paper, work in pairs to determine the answer, and then hold the cards up in an every-pupil-response format.
4. After having students answer questions about the words, you may choose to review some key terms by enlisting the aid of the class in discussing the meaning.
5. Next, ask the class prediction questions such as "Which word or words tell you about the main character? or Which word or words suggest if this is fiction or non-fiction?"
6. Write the predictions on the board or overhead to guide the students and focus their attention while reading.
7. Then, after reading, have the class return to the predictions to make modifications using as many of the terms as possible.
8. To further reinforce the vocabulary knowledge, you can review each word and ask students to locate a sentence where it is used in the story and what they think it means in that context.

Example: Sample Vocabulary, Language, and Prediction (VLP) Lesson

LANGUAGE ARTS

Story: Justin Lebo (Hoose, 1993)

I. Vocabulary

Justin Lebo	Kilbarchen Home for Boys
gunky	wheelies
inspecting	pirouettes
junker	passion
satisfaction	determined
realign	twenty-one
Father	assembly line
challenge	interchangeable
garage sales	donate
orphan	newspaper
publicity	interviews
bicycles	adjust

II. Language

For each area, ask questions such as the following:

Synonyms:
Which word means the same as "give"? *donate*
Which word means the same as "resolute" or
"with an intense purpose"? *determined*

Antonyms:
Which word means the opposite of a feeling of disinterest? *passion*

Categorization:
Group all the words that have to do with fixing things.
    realigned, adjust, inspecting, interchangeable
Group all the words that deal with tricks on a bicycle: *wheelies, pirouettes*
Context: I am looking forward to running the 5K because it
will _____ me. *challenge* The puppy is an _____ ; it was left by its
parents at an early age. *orphan*

Dictionary Usage: Using your dictionaries, find the definition of *publicity* as used in this sentence: "There was a great deal of publicity about the Steelers playing in the Super Bowl." Definition: *information about a person, thing, or event brought to notice or public attention*

Semantic Analysis: Which word fits in this sentence?
In order to build the boat, they each took a job and made an _____ to put the parts together. *assembly line*

Parts of Speech: Which words are verbs or show action?
inspecting; realign; donate; determined; interviews
Which words name something?
garage sales, bicycles, newspaper

Phonic Analysis: In which word(s) do you find the same sound of *u* as in "uncle"? *gunky, junker*

Structural Analysis: Which word(s) has a prefix meaning "between" or "among"? *interchangeable*
Which word has a prefix meaning "to do again"? *realign*

Rhyming Words: Which word rhymes with "spunky"? *gunky*

III. Prediction

Characterization
T: Which words probably tell you about the main character(s)?
     What can you predict about the characters?
S1: Justin Lebo; father
S2: Justin is 21 and is an orphan.
S3: His father is his foster father.

Setting
T: Which words tell you about where this story may be taking place?
S1: It is probably taking place somewhere they fix bicycles like a garage because it talks about realigning and adjusting.
S2: Or, it could take place at the boys' home.

Mood or feeling
T: Do any words tell you about the mood of the story?
S1: I think it is serious because it has words like *challenge* and *determined.*

Reality/fantasy
T: Do you think the story will be a fantasy or a reality?
S1: It will be a real story because it talks about the home for boys.
S2: Yes, and because it uses real words like *newspaper* and *bicycle.*

Events/outcomes

T: Which words give you clues about the events of the story? Use the words in a few sentences to predict some events and happenings.

S1: Since the stories we are reading deal with great things kids have done, I think Justin Lebo does something great with bicycles and tricks, like wheelies and pirouettes.

S2: I think he fixes bikes on an assembly line and donates them to someone.

S3: He gets a lot of newspaper interviews and publicity because of his bicycles.

IV. Reading stage

Have students read the passage focusing on the key words and determine if their predictions are confirmed or refuted.

V. Modifying predictions and vocabulary review

As a whole class, return to the predictions; then use the key words in sentences reflecting the actual content of the selection. An example is shown for characterization.

S1: *Justin Lebo* has a passion for fixing bicycles. He and his father take *junkers, realign* and *adjust* them.

(You can prompt the review by asking questions such as: "Who can show us where the word "interchangeable" was used? What sentence could we make with that word that reflects the story we read?")

S1: I found it on p. 125. It says "They were common bikes, and all the parts were *interchangeable.*"

S2: Because the parts were interchangeable, Justin could use old junker bikes to make like new ones.

Reprinted with permission from the National Middle School Association from: Wood, K. D., Harmon, J., & Hedrick, W. (2004). Recommendations from the research for teaching vocabulary to diverse learners. *Middle School Journal, 35*(5), 57-63.

S-31

INCIDENTAL MORPHEME METHOD

Developed by Manzo and Manzo (1990), the Incidental Morpheme Method capitalizes on students' existing knowledge of word roots and affixes to help them transfer and apply this knowledge to figure out the meanings of new words. Manzo and Manzo describe this method as "on-the-spot" instruction, which should be used for particular terms that warrant this type of attention. Not all content-specific words contain meaningful word parts that can be displayed in this manner.

Materials
Student notebooks for copying terms

Content Areas
All

Procedure

1. When selecting terms to pre-teach, notice any terms that may contain familiar word roots or affixes.
2. Display the term on the chalkboard or an overhead projector by dividing it into its meaningful word parts. For example, the term *hydrology* is displayed in the following manner:

    hydro   logy

3. Point to each word part and ask the students if they know what each part means. When a student provides the correct information, write the meaning under each part.
4. If students do not know the meanings of the word parts, then under each part, write clue words that may be familiar to the students.

	hydro	*logy*
Clue:	hydrant dehydrate	biology

5. Discuss the meanings of the clue words, and ask students to predict the meaning of the target word.
6. If students need more support, tell them the meaning of the root word and affix.

	hydro	*logy*	
Clue:	hydrant dehydrate	biology	**Meaning:** water, study of

7. Using the information you have provided, ask students to predict the literal meaning of the targeted word. Then provide a more detailed meaning if necessary.

> **Literal Meaning:** Hydrology is the study of water.
> **Detailed Meaning:** Hydrology is the scientific study of the properties, distribution, and effects of water on the earth's surface, in the soil and underlying rocks, and in the atmosphere.

8. Have students copy both definitions in their notebook.

Variations

- Maintain a word wall containing the words and terms that have the same roots and affixes.
- Have students keep a personal word wall sheet in a section of their notebooks to use as a future reference source.

S-32

ANIMAL CREATIONS

Adapted from the work of Johnson and Pearson (1984) and Cecil and Gipe (2003), Animal Creations allows students to apply their knowledge of affixes and roots that are frequently found in scientific terms. Students are given the task of creating an imaginary creature that can be identified by its scientific name.

Materials
Chart paper, sentence strips, markers, handout containing affixes and roots

Content Area
Science

Procedure
1. Provide students with a list of affixes and roots (see blackline master, p. 115).
2. Have students think of scientific terms that contain the affixes and roots.
3. Students now name a unique creature by selecting some of the affixes and roots on the list. Students write the scientific name on a sentence strip.
4. Once they have written the name, students draw a visual representation of this creature on the top two-thirds of a sheet of chart paper.
5. On the bottom of the chart paper, students write a statement connecting their creature to one of the real scientific terms containing similar affixes and roots.
6. Ask students to share their work.

Example: Lineatusbicornis monocephalustquadropod

My creature, Lineatusbicornis *mono*cephalustquadropod, has no problem using a *monocular* microscope.

Variations
• Have students work in groups to design their animal creations.
• Instead of creating animals, direct students to use the affixes and roots to create habitats for creatures.
• Have students omit the statements on their chart paper. Then display the drawings on one wall of the classroom. Have each student tell the name of the creature as he or she holds up a sentence strip. Direct the other students to guess which creature is represented by the sentence strip.

(Blackline Master)

COMMON AFFIXES AND ROOTS

macro – large, long	auri – ear	cephalus – head
vor – eat	tri – three	corp – body
melano – black	lineatus – lined	hepto – seven
uni – one	bruno – brown	micro – small
nano – billionth	quadro – four	poly – many
non – nine	chloro – green	rhino – nose
intra – within	derm – skin	-let – small
peri – around	glot – tongue	cornis – horn
poly – many	hex – six	cord, cardi – heart
leuco – white	punctata – dotted	-kin – small
bi – two	ocu – eye	-ling – small
erythro – red	pento – five	-trix – female
quint – five	pedi, pod – foot	mono – one
semi – half	dent, dont – tooth	ortho – straight
alb – white	dec – ten	-ician – person who

Instructional Strategies for Teaching Content Vocabulary, Grades 4-12, by Janis M. Harmon, Karen D. Wood, and Wanda B. Hedrick. Published by National Middle School Association and International Reading Association. Copyright 2006 by National Middle School Association.

S-33

MORPHEME CIRCLES

Morpheme Circles strategy, an adaptation of the Concept Circle activity (Vacca & Vacca, 2005), encourages students to think critically and conceptually about words that contain similar morphemes. This activity enables students to explore the relationships among words using a visually appealing format.

Materials
Handout containing Morpheme Circles

Content Areas
All

Procedure
1. After selecting the terms that students need to know, examine them for common morphemes.
2. Consider the meaning of the targeted morpheme and then list two or three related words containing the same morpheme. For example, if the term selected is *geography,* other words containing *graph* could be *cartography, biography,* and *photography.*
3. Develop a morpheme circle by writing the targeted word in one quadrant and then directing students to complete the other quadrants with related words.

Example
Complete the following morpheme circle with other words containing the root *graph.* Then below the circle, explain how the word meanings are related. All four words have something to do with writing or describing.

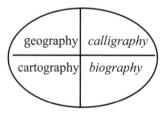

Variations
- Develop a morpheme circle using three words having the same root. Write each word in a quadrant and leave the fourth quadrant blank. Have students complete the fourth quadrant with the meaning of the root.
- Develop a morpheme circle using three related words and one unrelated word. Have students shade the word that is unrelated in meaning to the other three words.
- Have students create their own morpheme circles and then exchange with a partner to complete the activity.

(Blackline Master)

MORPHEME CIRCLES

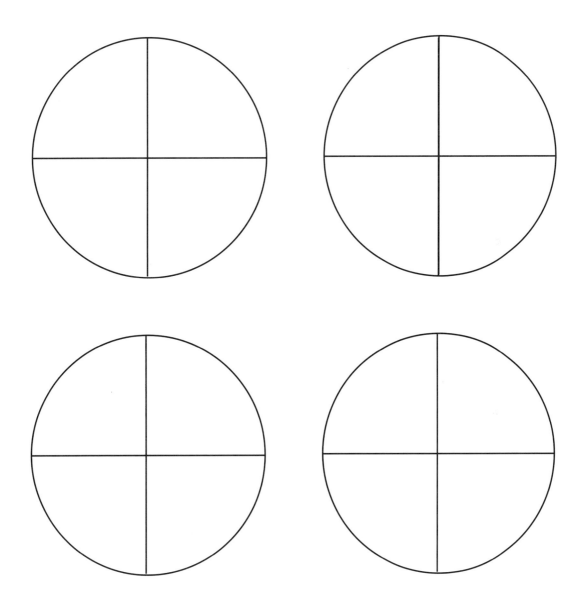

Instructional Strategies for Teaching Content Vocabulary, Grades 4-12, by Janis M. Harmon, Karen D. Wood, and Wanda B. Hedrick. Published by National Middle School Association and International Reading Association. Copyright 2006 by National Middle School Association.

S-34

WORD ORIGINS

The explanation of a word's origin can allow one to place the word in a setting so that it can be remembered. By learning a word or phrase, we can simply file it into categories, such as medicine, sports, or politics. Three reasons why students should study word origins are: (1) to develop word consciousness, (2) to develop an interest in word study, and (3) to provide additional contexts for word learning. (Dale, O'Rourke, & Bamman, 1971).

Materials
List of words to be researched,
Internet access, sentence strips of paper

Content Areas
All

Procedure
1. Introduce word origins to the class by showing examples.
2. Write the words that the students will be researching on the board or use an overhead.
3. Use the first word as an example as to how the assignment should be completed.
4. Students should use dictionaries and the Internet (see Web sites below) in order to do their research.
5. Encourage students to use sentence strips (when necessary) to divide the words into parts so that they can see the prefixes and suffixes that go into each word. They can work in groups, pairs, or individually.
6. Upon completion, students should have sentence strips for each word when necessary and a list of the words and their origins.

Web sites for Research

- http://www.westegg.com/etymology/
  A Web site of word origins in English, German, and French

- http://www.etymologic.com/
  An etymology game Web site

- http://www.yaelf.com/questions.shtml
  Word origins and their history

- http://www.wordwizard.com/
  A Web site for "lovers of the English Language." This site allows the user to search for word origins and their meanings.

- http://www.etymonline.com/
  An online etymology dictionary

Example: Sample Word Origins Lesson

1. Introduce word origins to the students with the following examples:
   - Sports probably began as a part of training for battle.
   - The Italian word for fresh is *fresco*, which gives us the name of a painting done on fresh plaster.
   - The diesel engine is named after Rudolph Diesel, a German engineer.
   - The Magna Carta (Latin for "Great Charter") is a document signed by King John at Runnymede in 1215 to give the English barons constitutional rights and privileges.
   - *Bisect* means cut in two (bi, two + sect, cut).
   - *Dissect* means cut apart (dis, apart + sect, cut).

2. Provide the following words for students to research (parentheses indicate origin):

tailor (clothesmaker)	cooper (barrelmaker)	cantor (singer)
crocker (cowherd)	furber (polisher)	flanner (cakemaker)
gaylor (jailor)	sears (carpenter)	proctor (attorney)
Rome (Romulus)	sandwich (Earl of Sandwich)	
pasteurize (Louis Pasteur)	cologne (Cologne, Germany)	

(Dale, O'Rourke, & Bamman, 1971)

3. The Internet contains multiple sites where games, dictionaries, and other word origin ideas are given. Students can test their knowledge of word origins by playing games.

Variations

- Have students work in pairs to make a matching game for another pair to test their knowledge of word origins.
- Provide words where the meaning has changed.

Examples

Minister once meant servant.

Spinster used to mean a woman who spins wool. Now it is a woman who is unmarried.

Cunning once meant knowing. Now it means possessing a sly kind of knowledge.

- Students can list the days of the week and months of the year and find their origin.
- Students can study Greek and Roman gods by finding the origin of their names and how they apply to the world today.
- Students can list the planets of the solar system and find their origin.

S-35

WHERE IN THE WORLD DID THAT WORD COME FROM?

According to Tompkins (2003), the English language began in 447AD when several tribes invaded England. Over the years the English language has been influenced by the inclusion of words from other languages. The study of the history of words provides interesting information about those words. The dictionary and the Internet are sources of information about the background of words. In the activity "Where in the World Did That Word Come From?" students use such Web sites as >http://www.etymonline.com< to find where a particular word originated and how it has changed over time after being introduced into the English language. Note that this activity is really not about the definition of the word directly, and if the students need that information they can use another Web site such as >http://www.dictionary.com< to find direct meaning-oriented information.

Materials
Internet access

Content Areas
All

Procedure

1. Ask students to find three words that are about a topic from a content area text source. Have them place the words in a chart under the column words. It is best if students do not have to look up more than three words to prevent boredom and have the activity become too labor intensive.
2. Have them predict two things about each word and place them in the columns called "My Guess." The first prediction is about where the word might have originated as used in the text. The second prediction is about how many years ago the word was first used.
3. Have students look up the word on the Internet Web site >http://www. etymonline.com<. After they find the word, they fill in the columns. "The Reality" columns include where the word originated and how long ago it was first used.
4. Have students cut and paste and save the Web site explanations, placing them in a notebook along with their predictions for later use and to add to their history of interesting words collection.
5. In the column entitled "How are the parts of the word explained?" students take information from the search, pull out the information that pertains to that question, and add to the column.
6. Have students share their word choices, predictions, and real meanings with other students.

Example

The word	Where in the world did it come from?		How old is the word?		How are the parts of the word explained?
	MY GUESS	IN REALITY	MY GUESS	IN REALITY	
electric	American	English, Latin, and Greek	150 years ago	350 years ago	"electrum" is Latin for amber and "electron" is Greek for amber. The forces were first done by rubbing amber. But I don't know what amber is.
volt	German	Named after a physicist "Volta"-Did not list his nationality	125 years ago	132 years ago	Word is from guy that discovered it—his last name.
current	English	Old French, Latin, Greek, and Old Norse	125 years ago	250 years ago	This one confused me but I think it comes from a word that is Old French "corant" that means running.

Search results as they appeared on Web site search >http://www.etymonline.com<

electric: 1646, first used in Eng. by Eng. physician Sir Thomas Browne (1605-1682), coined in Mod.L. by Eng. physicist William Gilbert (1540-1603) in treatise *De Magnete* (1600), from L. *electrum* "amber," from Gk. *elektron,* so called because the force was first generated by rubbing amber. *Electric toothbrush* first recorded 1936; *electric typewriter* 1958. *Electricity* is 1646, also in Browne's work. *Electrical* is first attested 1635; *electrify* in the figurative sense is from 1752.

volt: c.1873, back-formation from *voltaic* (1813), formed in allusion to Italian physicist Alessandro *Volta* (1745-1826), who perfected a chemical process used in electrical batteries. *Voltage* is first attested 1890.

current (adj): c.1300, from O.Fr. *corant* "running," prp. of *corre* "to run," from L. *currere* "to run," from PIE *kers- "to run" (cf. Gk. *-khouros* "running," Lith. *karsiu* "go quickly," O.N. *horskr* "swift," O.Ir., M.Welsh *carr* "cart, wagon," Bret. *karr* "chariot," Welsh *carrog* "torrent"). The noun is c.1380, from M.Fr. *corant,* from O.Fr. *corant.* Applied 1747 to the flow of electrical force. *Currently* "at the present time" is 1580.

Variations

- An easier variation would be to limit the words or to supply the words to be searched yourself.
- More information can be requested in a few additional columns, e.g., "Has the word ever been used as slang or some other meaning not clearly connected to the meaning found in the students' text source for the word? And if so, how?" or "List other words that come up in your search as related to the word."
- Use the above variation, but allow for group discussion. Allow the groups to create a "slang" use for one of the words they have searched that would be feasible. For example, the word "volt" listed in the example (p. 121) could be put into an expression like "Don't volt me!" and it might mean that the person is asking someone not to push him or her around.

(Blackline Master)

WHERE IN THE WORLD DID THAT WORD COME FROM?

The word	Where in the world did it come from?		How old is the word?		How are the parts of the word explained?
	My guess	In reality	My guess	In reality	

Instructional Strategies for Teaching Content Vocabulary, Grades 4-12, by Janis M. Harmon, Karen D. Wood, and Wanda B. Hedrick. Published by National Middle School Association and International Reading Association. Copyright 2006 by National Middle School Association.

—7—

Monitoring and Assessing Content Word Learning

Metacognition, the ability to think about one's own thinking and learning, applies to all areas of learning including content area vocabulary. The seven strategies described in this chapter provide the structure students need to monitor their vocabulary development in the content areas as well as periodically assess what they know and need to know about specific topics. These activities can empower students to become supervisors of their own learning as they interact with new words and meanings in the content areas. Furthermore, the activities identified below foster independent word learning habits that can transfer to word learning in a variety of areas.

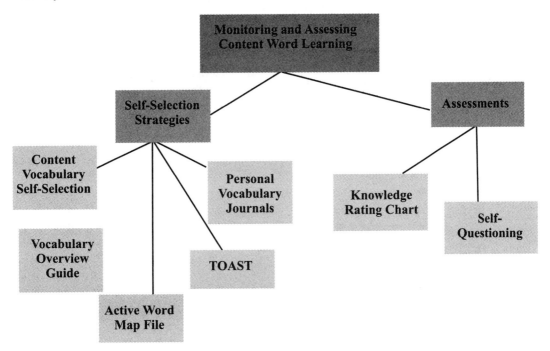

S-36

CONTENT VOCABULARY SELF-SELECTION

The Content Vocabulary Self-Selection activity is an adaptation of Haggard's (1986) vocabulary self-collection procedure that is widely promoted by experts in the field of reading. Vocabulary self-collection heightens word awareness by directing student teams to find words in their reading that they think all students in the class should learn. Students and the teacher discuss the targeted words and then collectively agree on which words should be on the class list. In this adaptation, students work independently to find words, in small groups to discuss words, and in a whole class format to teach their self-selected words to all students in the class.

Materials
Assigned text passages, paper, pens

Content Areas
All

Procedure

1. Find three or four passages addressing a topic that the class is studying. Divide students into several groups depending upon the number of passages being used.
2. Students individually read assigned passages and highlight words they think are important to understanding the passage.
3. Have students complete a two-column chart with these headings: (1) WORDS SELECTED and (2) REASONS FOR SELECTING THE WORDS.
4. Once students have completed this, direct them to get together with others reading the same passage to compare their word lists. In this group students talk about their words and decide on five or six words they think everyone should know and learn.
5. Groups then complete a two-column chart with headings (1) words selected and (2) reasons for selecting the words.
6. Have group members with the same topic subdivide into two groups to prepare for the teaching section of the activity. One group will develop a PowerPoint presentation of important information about the passage using the highlighted terms. This group will also submit questions for a quiz. The other group will create a word game with the targeted words (e.g, Tic Tac Toe, I have…Who has…) and submit five meaningful questions for the quiz.
7. Allow class time for presentations and interactive word games.

Example

In a class study of the Holocaust, one group of students read a passage about Nazi propaganda. After discussing self-selected words, the group decided to include the words listed below in its presentation.

Words to include in presentation	Why they are important
propaganda	The Nazis used this to influence the people. They used magazines and music to brainwash Germans.
anti-Semitism	Nazis were against Jews and they were trying to get children to learn that.
atrocities	This is how the United States and other Jews thought about the deaths.
Hitler	He was the main leader of the Nazis and inflicted major damage on the Jews.
pure	Someone with no Jewish blood.
censorship	They burned the books and stuff that had to do with the Jews.

Possible questions for the quiz:

Would Hitler consider homeless people to be racially *pure*?

Would a song by a popular "pure" German singer be *censored* in Nazi Germany?

Many things that Hitler and the Nazis did to the Jews showed *anti-Semitism* because

_____.

The Nazis conducted many *propaganda* campaigns with the German people, because _____.

Variations

1. Find several passages related to a similar topic. Group students by passage and then have them come together to discuss words that describe the larger topic.
2. Use heterogeneous groups so that English Language Learners and other students with special needs will have an opportunity to participate in the activities.
3. Have students evaluate the activities and assess their own learning.

Worksheet #1

Name: _____   Date: _____

Class: _____

Text: _____

Words a reader needs to know to understand this passage:	Reasons why readers need to know these words:

Worksheet #2:   **Small Group Information Sheet**

Name: _____   Date: _____

Class: _____

Text: _____

Words that group members believe everyone should know:	Why everyone should know this word:

Instructional Strategies for Teaching Content Vocabulary, Grades 4-12, by Janis M. Harmon, Karen D. Wood, and Wanda B. Hedrick. Published by National Middle School Association and International Reading Association. Copyright 2006 by National Middle School Association.

(Blackline Master)

Worksheet #3:   **Information Sheet for PowerPoint Presentation**

Name: _____   **Date:** _____

Class: _____

Text: _____

Directions:

1. What would you like to include in your presentation? Talk this over with the group members. Decide in what order the information should be in the slide presentation.
2. Use the words you selected and the information from the passages to complete the table below.
3. Underline the words you selected.

Slide Number	Information (Underline selected vocabulary words.)
#1	
#2	
#3	
#4	
#5	
#6	

S-37

VOCABULARY OVERVIEW GUIDE

The Vocabulary Overview Guide developed by Carr (1985) helps students monitor their vocabulary meaning constructions as they read a text. The students are asked to self-select words they think are important for understanding a passage and then consider word meaning possibilities from the context. They also check definitions in a glossary or dictionary, decide on related categories, and select clues for remembering the word meaning. This information will help the students as they study the words.

Materials
Vocabulary Overview Map

Content Areas
All

Procedure

1. Provide students with a blank Vocabulary Overview Guide and explain that its purpose is to help them study the concepts of a chapter by focusing on important vocabulary.
2. Direct students to use these steps:
   a. Skim the text to identify the topic, and flag unfamiliar vocabulary with sticky notes.
   b. For each word, read the context carefully to determine any word meaning clues. Jot down the context clues on a sticky note and predict the meaning.
   c. Refer to the glossary or dictionary to verify your prediction.
   d. Decide on a category for the word. Write the category on the sticky note.
   e. Write the category at the top of the guide and then write the word under that column.
   f. Complete the entry by writing the definition of the word and any clue words to help you remember the meaning.
3. Students continue to use the steps above for each new term, adding different categories to the guide and using it to study the definitions and clues as they review each term.

Example: Vocabulary Overview Guide on Geography of the Americas

TOPIC: GEOGRAPHY OF THE AMERICAS

Category: Landforms	**Category:** People	**Category:** Resources	**Category:** Economy
Word: tundra **Clue**: No trees **Meaning:** rolling plain without trees found in Arctic	**Word:** bilingual **Clue:** Canadians who speak French and English **Meaning**: referring to two languages	**Word:** wood pulp **Clue:** paper **Meaning:** wet, ground-up chips of wood	**Word**: inflation **Clue**: Buy less with your money **Meaning:** A decrease in the value of money as prices for goods and services increase
Word: prairie **Clue:** Wheat grows there. **Meaning:** rolling land with tall grasses and fertile soil	**Word**: immigrant **Clue:** Most Americans **Meaning**: person who moves to one country from another country to live permanently	**Word:** renewable resource **Clue:** trees **Meaning**: resources that can be replaced after being used	**Word:** capital **Clue**: poor countries have little money **Meaning**: money needed for a country to develop
Word: coastal plain **Clue:** harbors and shipping **Meaning:** flat land bordering a coast	**Word:** Hispanic **Clue:** My friend Juan **Meaning:** American ethnic group that speaks Spanish		**Word:** regional specialization **Clue:** Fishing in New England **Meaning:** a special activity of a region that helps the economy
	Word: Mestizo **Clue:** People in north and central Mexico **Meaning:** Person whose ancestors are both European and American Indian		

Variations

- Have students list all words and define them. Then direct them to separate the words into possible categories.
- Add another section to the map to include word part analysis where students can identify known prefixes or roots.

(Blackline Master)

VOCABULARY OVERVIEW GUIDE
(adapted from Carr (1985)

Topic: _____

Category	Category	Category	Category
Word: _____ Clue: _____ Meaning: ___ ___ ___ ___	Word: _____ Clue: _____ Meaning: ___ ___ ___ ___	Word: _____ Clue: _____ Meaning: ___ ___ ___ ___	Word: _____ Clue: _____ Meaning: ___ ___ ___ ___
Word: _____ Clue: _____ Meaning: ___ ___ ___ ___	Word: _____ Clue: _____ Meaning: ___ ___ ___ ___	Word: _____ Clue: _____ Meaning: ___ ___ ___ ___	Word: _____ Clue: _____ Meaning: ___ ___ ___ ___

S-38

ACTIVE WORD MAP FILE

The Active Word Map File helps students, especially English Language Learners, monitor their own vocabulary development through the use of an ongoing, open file for words. Adapted from Anderson and Roit's Vocabulary Networking (1996), the Active Word Map file consists of a collection of word maps organized around various categories selected by the student. The open-ended nature of the files allows students to add to the mappings as they encounter related words and ideas about the targeted words in subsequent readings or class discussions.

Materials
Blank word maps

Content Areas
All

Procedure

1. Explain to students the purpose of the Active Word Map File and that, because they are the CEOs of their own learning, they can take charge of their vocabulary development. Mention that because word learning is incremental, we continually learn something new about a word in nearly every encounter with the word.

2. Direct students to select one or two words that they think are important for understanding the topic being discussed in class.

3. Provide a blank word map for the students. Brainstorm possible categories that students can use in their maps. Some examples of categories include the following: description of word, examples and non-examples, cognates, synonyms and antonyms, words typically used with the targeted word, contexts for using the word, analysis of word parts, related people, places, events, and ideas, impressions about the word, and text references.

4. Direct students to select at least three categories to begin their file. Once they have completed the file, remind them that they must periodically add more information to the maps and indicate where they found this information.

Examples: History example: Dwight Eisenhower

English example: idioms

HISTORY—DWIGHT EISENHOWER

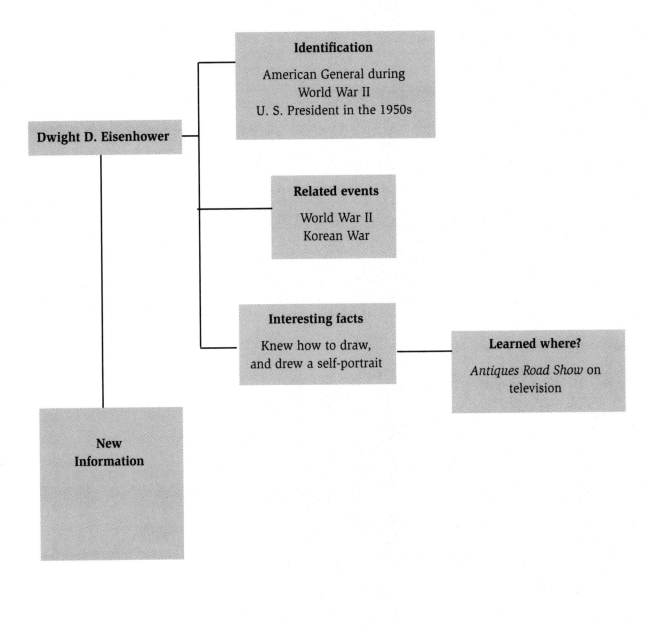

ENGLISH—LEGEND

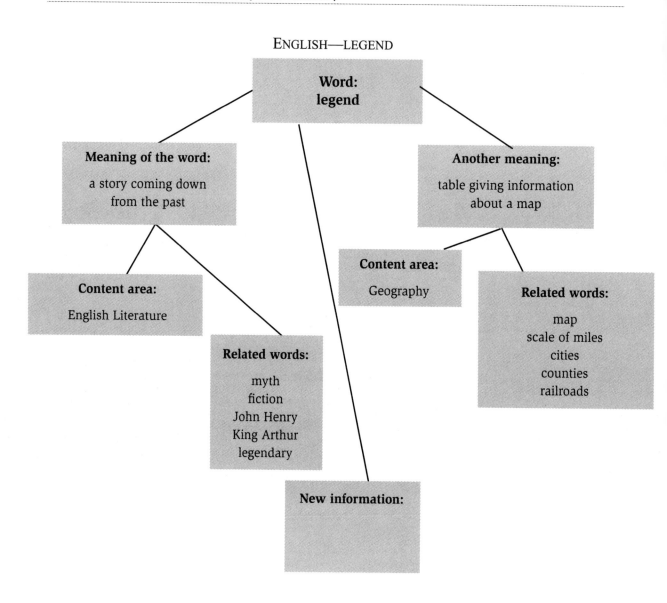

Variations

- Initially provide a blank map with general categories. Once students understand how the maps work, then they should be able to develop their own.
- Students can code polysemous words by color to indicate different meanings in different content areas.
- Students can work with partners to review what they know about their words.
- Students can refer to their open files when writing.
- The open-ended features enable students to periodically assess their knowledge about particular words.
- Students can use the computer in creating their maps.

S-39

TOAST: AN INDEPENDENT WORD LEARNING STUDY STRATEGY

Dana and Rodriguez (1992) developed a useful strategy called TOAST to help students study new vocabulary terms. The acronym TOAST stands for *test, organize, anchor, say,* and *test.* This procedure provides students with a systematic way for learning and remembering new and unfamiliar terms. Because of its potential for wide application across content areas, this strategy can become part of a student's repertoire of valuable study strategies.

Materials
List of vocabulary words, index cards, paper

Content Areas
All

Procedure
1. Introduce the strategy by showing students that TOAST is an acronym for *Test, Organize, Anchor, Say,* and *Test.*
2. Explain the purpose of each part using the following descriptions:
   - **Test**: Students begin by self-testing to determine which words are familiar and which ones need to be studied. Once students have compiled their list of words, they develop flash cards by writing the word on one side of an index card and the meaning on the other side. They can use the flash cards by themselves or with a partner to acquire mastery.
   - **Organize**: To facilitate learning, students need to examine the list of words for possible categories that can illustrate connections and relationships among the words. They can then develop a visual representation of these relationships.
   - **Anchor**: To internalize word meanings, students need to make connections and relate the word to other words. They also need multiple exposures using the words. Possible ways to "anchor" word meanings can be the following: (1) develop a list of related words; (2) review with a partner; (3) create some type of mnemonic device to help with recall; (4) look for familiar parts in the word; and (5) practice using the word in a meaningful context.
   - **Say**: Students need to reinforce and review the word meanings frequently. Review sessions should occur the same day the words are introduced and then periodically until the test.
   - **Test**: After each review session, students need to self-test again to determine if they know the words. They can use the flash cards developed with the pretest.

Example
The example provided is a guide that students can use to learn the strategy. This guide can also be enlarged in poster format to hang on the classroom wall as a reminder for students.

TOAST

Independent Word Learning Study Strategy

Test
- Test yourself. What words do you know? What words do you need to study?
- Make index cards writing the word on one side and the meaning on the other side.

Organize
- Examine your word list.
- Look for connections and relationships among the words.
- Find categories.
- Develop a word map using these categories.

Anchor
- Ask yourself: "I cannot talk about this word without talking about _____."
  Then write a list of related words.
- Create a mnemonic device to remember the word meaning.
- Look for familiar word parts.
- Practice using the word in a meaningful way with a partner.

Say
- Review the word meanings right after learning them.
- Review the word meanings every day until the test.

Test
- Test yourself after each review session.
- Use the flash cards from the pretest.

Variations

- Model the strategy with a list of words so that students, especially English Language Learners, can understand what to do.
- Provide a variety of suggestions to help students with the "anchor" step.
  These suggestions can include dramatizing word meanings or drawing visual representations of the word or related words.

S-40

PERSONAL VOCABULARY JOURNALS

Another way to promote active learning and monitor understanding is through the use of self-selected vocabulary. So often the vocabulary terms students learn are words chosen by the teacher or suggested by commercially prepared materials and textbooks. The Personal Vocabulary Journal (Wood, 1994; Wood & Harmon, 2002) can be applied to any content area because it allows students to self-select their own vocabulary terms by focusing on new words in the classroom or in other environments away from school.

Materials
Varied sources related to the topic under study

Content Areas
All

Procedure

1. Set the purposes for the journal by asking students if they have ever heard or read a word—in school or out—and wondered what it meant. Also, suggest the benefits of choosing their own vocabulary words to study instead of learning words as determined by the teacher.
2. Show students a blank Personal Vocabulary Journal form—either as a handout or on the overhead. Tell the students that they will use this form to record one or more new words related to the current unit of study or ones that they find interesting.
3. Demonstrate a sample entry by "thinking aloud" the means by which students would select and record a new word. Encourage class participation during this step.
4. Students can be assigned to small groups to share their choice of words from their vocabulary journals. When appropriate, they may be asked to "act out" their words or make a drawing showing its meaning.
5. Also, students can select two or three words from their collection for weekly or unit quizzes. These terms would be submitted to the teacher for assessment purposes.
6. Students can use the words in composing a passage to give them practice in usage and application.

Examples

Personal Vocabulary Journal: Examples from *The Cay* (Taylor, 1969)

Sample One

My new word is: mutiny

It is related to: Phillip's father, his work, and the Chinese

I found it in: *The Cay* on pg. 21, Ch.2

The sentence where I found it: They were angry with the Chinese crews, and on the third day, my father said that mutiny charges had been placed against them.

I think it means: criminal charges

The context clues I used were: charges placed against them; against usually means bad

The appropriate dictionary definition is: open rebellion against constituted authority, especially rebellion of sailors against superior officers

It reminds me of: a person on trial for breaking the law

My sentence is: There was mutiny on the ship when the sailors didn't agree with the commands they were given.

Sample Two

My new word is: refinery

It is related to: oil

I found it in: *The Cay* on pg. 9, Ch.1; it appeared for the first time here. When I came across it I skipped over it, and then there it was on page 10; so I decided I better look it up. It appears many more times throughout the book.

The sentence where I found it: I remember that on that moonless night in February 1942 they attacked the big Logo Oil refinery on Aruba, the sister island west of us.

I think it means: building, factory

The context clues I used were: make into gasoline, kerosene, and diesel oil

The appropriate dictionary definition is: an industrial plant for purifying a crude substance, such as petroleum or sugar

It reminds me of: Cannon Mills and my dad making towels

My sentence is: The refinery down the road from my house always smells of gas fumes.

*Examples reprinted with permission of Guilford Press from Wood, K., & Mraz, M. (2005). *Teaching literacy in the sixth grade.* New York: Guilford.

(Blackline Master)

PERSONAL VOCABULARY JOURNAL

My new word is: _____

It is related to: _____

I found it in: _____

The sentence where I found it: _____

I think it means: _____

The context clues I used were: _____

The appropriate dictionary definition: _____

It reminds me of: _____

My sentence is: _____

S-41

KNOWLEDGE RATING CHART

The Knowledge Rating Chart (Blachowicz & Fisher, 2002) is an activity designed to help students evaluate what they know and do not know about specific terms. It can serve as a pre-reading activity to develop students' metacognitive awareness about word meanings and as a post-reading activity to help students assess their own learning.

Materials
Knowledge Rating Chart

Content Areas
All

Procedure

1. Select the vocabulary terms for a text passage. Include the terms in the first column of the Knowledge Rating Chart and also display the terms on the chalkboard or overhead projector.

2. Pronounce the words for the students and then ask them to assess their knowledge of each term. Explain what each column heading represents. Your explanations may be similar to the following: "I know this word" means that you can define the word and use it in your speaking and writing. "The word looks familiar" means that you have probably heard of it before but you are not sure about its meaning. "I do not know this word" means that the word is totally unfamiliar to you.

3. Direct the students to place a check in the appropriate column. If they are familiar with the word, have them write a brief definition in that column.

4. Conduct a class discussion based upon the ratings. Have students who are familiar with the terms explain the meanings. Direct students to think about general categories for words, such the category "gas" for carbon dioxide.

5. Have students read the selection containing the words. Remind them to pay attention to how the author uses the words and to look for new information about the word.

6. After reading, direct students to complete the last column on the activity sheet.

7. Discuss student responses.

Example: Knowledge Rating Chart
World Geography

Word	I know this word (or phrase). It means...	The word (or phrase) looks familiar.	I do not know this word (or phrase).	New information from the text
region				
relief				
glacier				
plateau				
reservoir				
absolute location				
relative location				
tundra				
permafrost				
peninsula				

Variations

- Have students think of other or alternate column headings for the Knowledge Rating Chart.
- Conduct discussions of word meanings after reading instead of before reading. Then have students re-evaluate their understanding of the terms.

(Blackline Master)

KNOWLEDGE RATING CHART

(adapted from Blachowicz & Fisher, 2002)

Word	I know this word (or phrase). It means...	The word (or phrase) looks familiar.	I do not know this word (or phrase).	New information from the text

Instructional Strategies for Teaching Content Vocabulary, Grades 4-12, by Janis M. Harmon, Karen D. Wood, and Wanda B. Hedrick. Published by National Middle School Association and International Reading Association. Copyright 2006 by National Middle School Association.

S-42

SELF-QUESTIONING

Self-Questioning is an effective tool for helping students develop metalinguistic awareness and thus improve comprehension. It is especially important for helping struggling readers realize that they can make strategic decisions when encountering unfamiliar words in their reading.

Materials
Text

Content Areas
All

Procedure

1. Begin a class discussion by asking students what they do when they encounter an unfamiliar term while reading in a particular content area. Write student responses on the chalkboard or overhead projector.

2. Explain that it is important to ask yourself questions about the term in order to figure out the meaning.

3. Add the following questions to what the students have already mentioned:
   - Do I know this word?
   - Do I need to know this word to understand what I am reading?
     How do I know that it is important?
   - If I think this word is important, what do I already know about it?
   - What does the word have to do with what I am reading?
     What is it referring to?
   - How does the author use the word?
     Does it describe something or show action?
   - Do I see any word parts that make sense?
   - Do I know enough about this word?
   - Do I need more information?
   - How can I find out more about this word?
     Should I ask someone or use the dictionary?

   (Harmon, 2000. p. 525)

4. Write the questions on a chart and hang it in the classroom. Encourage students to refer to the chart when they encounter unfamiliar words in their reading.

(Blackline Master)

QUESTIONS TO ASK MYSELF WHEN I ENCOUNTER AN UNFAMILIAR WORD

- **Do I know this word?**

- **Do I need to know this word to understand what I am reading? How do I know that it is important?**

- **If I think this word is important, what do I already know about it?**

- **What does the word have to do with what I am reading? What is it referring to?**

- **How does the author use the word? Does it describe something or show action?**

- **Do I see any word parts that make sense?**

- **Do I know enough about this word?**

- **Do I need more information?**

- **How can I find out more about this word? Should I ask someone or use the dictionary?**

Instructional Strategies for Teaching Content Vocabulary, Grades 4-12, by Janis M. Harmon, Karen D. Wood, and Wanda B. Hedrick. Published by National Middle School Association and International Reading Association. Copyright 2006 by National Middle School Association.

References

Alvermann, D.E., & Phelps, S.F. (2002). *Content reading and literacy: Succeeding in today's diverse classrooms* (3rd ed.). Boston, MA: Allyn and Bacon.

Alvermann, D.E., & Phelps, S.F. (2005). *Content reading and literacy: Succeeding in today's diverse classrooms* (4th ed.). Boston: Allyn & Bacon.

Anderson, V., & Roit, M. (1996). Linking reading comprehension instruction to language development for language minority students. *Elementary School Journal, 96*(3), 295-309.

Baumann, J.F., Kameenui, E.J., & Ash, G.E. (2003). Research on vocabulary instruction: Voltaire redux. In J. Flook, D. Lapp, J.R. Squire, & J.M. Jensen (Eds.), *Handbook of research on teaching the English language arts* (pp. 752-785). Mahwah, NJ: Lawrence Erlbaum Associates.

Bean, T.W., Singer, H., Sorter, J., & Frasee, C. (1986). The effect of metacognitive instruction in outlining and graphic organizer construction on students' comprehension in a tenth-grade world history class. *Journal of Reading Behavior, 18,* 153-169. (ERIC Document Reproduction Service No. 393 484)

Beck, R.B., Black, L., Krieger, L.S., Naylor, P.C., & Shabaka, D.I. (1999). *World history: Patterns of interaction.* Evanston, IL: McDougal Littell.

Beck, I.L., McKeown, M.G., & Kucan, L. (2003). *Bringing words to life: Robust vocabulary instruction.* New York: Guilford Press.

Blachowicz, C., & Fisher, P. (2002). *Teaching vocabulary in all classrooms* (2nd ed.). Upper Saddle River, NJ: Merrill Prentice-Hall.

Blachowicz, C., & Fisher, P. (2006). Teaching vocabulary in all classrooms (3rd ed.). Upper Saddle River, NJ: Merrill Prentice-Hall.

Carr, E.M. (1985). The vocabulary overview guide: A metacognitive strategy to improve vocabulary comprehension and retention. *Journal of Reading, 28,* 684-689.

Cecil, N.L., & Gipe, J.P. (2003). *Literacy in the intermediate grades: Best practices for a comprehensive program.* Scottsdale, AZ: Holcomb Hathaway, Publishers.

Dale, E., O'Rourke, J., & Bamman, H.A. (1971). *Techniques of teaching vocabulary.* Atlanta, GA: Field Education Publications, Inc.

Dana, C., & Rodriguez, M. (1992). TOAST: A system to study vocabulary. *Reading Research and Instruction, 31*(4), 78-84.

Ellis, E. (1992). *LINCS: A starter strategy for vocabulary learning.* Lawrence, KS: Edge.

Foil, C.R., & Alber, S.R. (2002). Fun and effective ways to build your students' vocabulary. *Intervention in School & Clinic, 37,* 131-139.

Fry, E. B. (2004). *The teacher's book of lists.* San Francisco, CA: Jossey-Bass.

Gunning, T.G. (2004). *Creating literacy instruction for all students in grades 4 to 8.* Needham Heights, MA: Allyn & Bacon.

Haggard, M.R. (1986). The vocabulary self-collection strategy: Using student interest and word knowledge to enhance vocabulary growth. *Journal of Reading, 29,* 634-642.

Harmon, J.M. (2000). Assessing and supporting independent word learning strategies of middle school students. *Journal of Adolescent and Adult Literacy, 43*(6), 518-527.

Harmon, J.M., & Hedrick, W. B. (2000). Zooming In and Zooming Out: Enhancing vocabulary and conceptual learning in social studies. *The Reading Teacher, 54*(2), 155-159.

Harmon, J.M., & Hedrick, W. B. (2001). Zooming in and zooming out for better vocabulary learning. *Middle School Journal, 32*(5), 22-29.

Hatfield, C.B., Kelly-Coupar, P., Hoh, C., & Lindsey, A. (1998). *World Geography.* Parsippany, NJ: Silver Burdett Ginn.

Hoose, P. (1993) *Justin Lebo. It's our world too!* Boston: Little, Brown and Company.

Huffman, L.E. (2000). Spotlighting specifics by combining focus questions. In D.W. Moore, D.E. Alvermann, & K.A. Hinchman (Eds.), *Struggling adolescent readers: A collection of teaching strategies* (pp. 220-222). Newark, DE: International Reading Association.

Johnson, D.D. (2001). *Vocabulary in the elementary and middle school.* Needham Heights, MA: Allyn & Bacon.

Johnson, D.D., & Pearson, P.D. (1984). *Teaching reading vocabulary* (2nd ed.). New York: Holt, Rinehart and Winston.

Kostyal, K.M. (1999). *Trial by ice: A photobiography of Sir Ernest Shackleton.* New York: Scholastic, Inc.

Lederer, R. (1993, March). 56 B.C. and all that. *National Review, 45,* 51.

Manzo, A., & Manzo, U. (1990). *Content area reading: A heuristic approach.* Columbus, OH: Merrill Publishing Company.

Manzo, A.V., Manzo, U.C., & Thomas, M.M. (2005). *Content area literacy: Strategic teaching for strategic learning.* (4th ed.). Hoboken, NJ: John Wiley & Sons, Inc.

Marco, M., & Luzon, M.J. (1999). Procedural vocabulary: Lexical signaling of conceptual relations in discourse. *Applied Linguistics, 20*(1), 1-21.

Mastropieri, M.A., & Scruggs, T.E. (1998). Enhancing school success with mnemonic strategies. *Intervention in School & Clinic, 33,* 201-208.

McClenaghan, W.A. (1993). *Magruder's American government.* Needham, MA: Prentice Hall.

Merkely, D.M., & Jefferies, D. (2000/2001). Guidelines for implementing a graphic organizer. *The Reading Teacher, 54*(4), 350-357.

Middleton, J.L. (1991). Science-generated analogies in biology. *The American Biology Teacher, 53*(1), 42-46.

Moore, D.W., & Readence, J.E. (1984). A quantitative and qualitative review of graphic organizer research. *Journal of Educational Research, 78.* 11-17.

Nagy, W.E. (1988). *Teaching vocabulary to improve reading comprehension.* Newark, DE: International Reading Association.

Nagy, W.E., & Anderson, R.C. (1984). How many words are there in printed school English? *Reading Research Quarterly, 19,* 304-330.

Ogle, D.M. (1986). K-W-L: A teaching model that develops action reading of expository text. *The Reading Teacher, 40,* 564-570.

Paivio, A. (1990). *Mental representations: A dual coding approach.* New York: Oxford University Press.

Punch, M., & Robinson, M. (1992). Social studies vocabulary mnemonics. *Social Education 56*(7), 402-403.

Rasinski, T.V., & Padak, N.D. (2001). *From phonics to fluency: Effective teaching of decoding and reading fluency in the elementary school.* New York: Longman.

Readence, J.E., Bean, T.W., & Baldwin, R.S. (2000). *Content area literacy: An integrated approach.* Dubuque, IA: Kendall-Hunt Publishing Company.

Readence, J.E., Moore, D.W., & Rickelman, R.J. (2000). *Prereading activities for content area reading and learning.* Newark, DE: International Reading Association.

Strategies for Effective Literacy Learning (n.d). Retrieved January 11, 2005, from http://www. d46.k12.il.us/curriculum/index.html

Schwartz, R.M. (1988). Learning to learn vocabulary in content area textbooks. *Journal of Reading, 32,* 108-118.

Schwartz, R.M. & Raphael, T.E. (1985). Concept of definition: A key to improving students' vocabulary. *Reading Teacher, 39,* 198-205.

Stahl, S. & Kapinus, B. A. (1991) Possible sentences: Prediction word meanings to teach content area vocabulary. *The Reading Teacher, 45,* 36-43.

Strong, R.W., Perini, M.J., Silver, H.F., & Tuculescu, G.M. (2002). *Reading for academic success: Powerful strategies for struggling, average, and advanced readers, grades 7-12.* Thousand Oaks, CA: Corwin Press, Inc.

Taylor, T. (1969). *The Cay.* Garden City, NY: Doubleday.

Tierney, R.J., and Readence, J.E. (2000). *Reading strategies and practices: A compendium* (5th ed.). Boston: Allyn & Bacon.

Tompkins, G. E. (2003). *Literacy for the 21st century.* Upper Saddle River, NJ: Merrill/ Prentice Hall.

Vacca, R.T., & Vacca, J.L. (2002). *Content area reading: Literacy and learning across the curriculum.* (7th ed.). Boston, MA: Allyn and Bacon.

Vacca, R.T., & Vacca, J.L. (2005). *Content area reading: Literacy and learning across the curriculum* (8th ed.). Boston: Allyn & Bacon.

Welker, W. (1987). Open to suggestion: Going from typical to technical meaning. *Journal of Reading, 31*(3), 275-276.

Wood, K. D. (1994). *Practical strategies for improving instruction.* Westerville, OH: National Middle School Association.

Wood, K. (2001). *Literacy strategies across the subject areas: Process-oriented blackline masters for the K-12 classroom.* Boston: Allyn and Bacon.

Wood, K.D., & Endres, C. (2005). Motivating student interest with the Imaging, Elaborate, Predict, and Confirm (IEPC) strategy. *The Reading Teacher, 58,* 2-14.

Wood, K.D., & Harmon, J.M. (2002). *Strategies for integrating reading and writing in middle and high school classrooms.* Westerville, OH: National Middle School Association.

Wood, K.D., & Mraz, M. (2005). *Teaching literacy in the sixth grade.* New York: Guilford.

Wood, K.D., Harmon, J., & Hedrick, W. (2004). Recommendations from the research for teaching vocabulary to diverse learners. *Middle School Journal, 35*(5), 57-63.

Wood, K.D., & Robinson, N. (1983). Vocabulary, language and prediction: A prereading strategy. *The Reading Teacher, 36* (4), 392-495.